B. P. Pratten

**Acts and Laws**

Passed by the great and general Court or Assembly of Their Majesties

Province of the Massachussets-Bay, in New England

B. P. Pratten

**Acts and Laws**
*Passed by the great and general Court or Assembly of Their Majesties Province of the Massachussets-Bay, in New England*

ISBN/EAN: 9783337191436

Printed in Europe, USA, Canada, Australia, Japan

Cover: Foto ©ninafisch / pixelio.de

More available books at **www.hansebooks.com**

# By His Excellency.

I Order Benjamin Harris to Print the Acts and Laws made by the Great and General Court, or Assembly of this Their Majesties Province of the Massachusetts-Bay in New-England, that so the People may be Informed thereof.

*Boston December 16th. 1692.*

William Phips.

# The Contents.

AN Act, setting forth General Priviledges Page 1

An Act, For the Quieting of Possessions, and Setling of Titles. pag. 2

An Act, For Building with Stone or Brick in the Town of Boston, and preventing Fire. pag. 4

An Act, For the Settling and Distribution of the Estates of Intestates. pag. 6

An Act, For prevention of Frauds and Perjuries. pag. 9

An Act, For the Equal Distribution of Insolvent Estates. pag. 12

An Act, For Regulating the Assize of Cask, and preventing Deceit in Packing of Fish, Beef, and Pork, for Sale. pag. 13

An Act, For Punishing of Criminal Offenders. pag. 16

An Act, For the Punishing of Capital Offenders. pag. 21

An Act, For the Suppressing of Unlicensed Houses, and the due Regulation of such as are, or shall be Licensed. pag. 26

An Act, For Impost and Excise. pag. 28

An Act, For the better Observation and keeping the Lords Day. ibid.

An Act, For Prevention of Common Nusances arising by Slaughter-Houses, Still-Houses, &c. Tallow Chandlers, and Curriers. pag. 30

An Act, For Affirming of Former Judgments, and providing for Executions. pag. 31

An Act, For the orderly Consumating of Marriages. pag. 33

An Act, For the Settlement and Support of Ministers and School-Masters. pag. 34

An Act For the Settlement of the Bounds, and defraying of the Publick and Necessary Charges arising within each Respective County in this Province. pag. 36

An Act For Regulating of Townships, Choice of Town Officers, and setting forth their Power pag. 37

An Act, For making of Lands and Tenements liable to the payment of Debts. pag. 43

An Act For due Regulation of weights and Measures. pag. 45

An Act, Against the Counterfeiting, Clipping, Rounding, Filing or impairing of Coins. pag. 47

An Act, For the Regulating and Encouragement of Fishery. pag. 48

An Act, For the Establishing of Judicatories and Courts of Justice, within this Province pag. 49

An Act, Requiring the Taking the Oaths, appointed to be taken instead of the Oaths of Allegiance, and Supremacy. pag. 56

An Act For the establishing of Forms of Oaths. pag. 58

An Act, For the Establishing of Presidents and Forms of Writs, and Processes. pag. 61

An Act For regulating Fees. pag. 69

An Act, For ascertaining the number, and regulating the House of Representatives pag. 75

An Act, For the Prevention of Danger by the French residing within this Province pag. 78

An Act, against Conjuration, Witchcraft, and dealing with evil and wicked Spirits. pag. 79

An Act, For regulating the former assessment and for granting an additional Supply of Money. pag. 80

An Act, For the better securing the liberty of the subject, and for prevention of illegal imprisonment. pag. 85

An Act for the reviving of an act for continuing of the Local Laws. And one other Act for sending of Souldiers to the relief of the Neighbouring Provinces, and Colonies pag. 90

An Act

# ACTS
## AND
# LAWS,

Passed by the Great and General Court or Assembly of Their Majesties Province of the Massachusets-Bay, in

## New-England.

Begun at *Boston*, the Eighth Day of *June*, 1692. And Continued by Adjournment, unto *Wednesday* the Twelfth Day of *October* following: Being the Second Sessions.

*Anno Regni Gulielmi, et Mariæ, Regis et Reginæ Angliæ, Scotiæ, Franciæ, et Hiberniæ, Quarto.*

*BOSTON*
Printed by *Benjamin Harris*, Printer to His Excellency, the Governour and Council, 1692.

# Acts and Laws,

Passed by the Great and General Court or Assembly of Their Majesties Province of the Massachusets-Bay, in New-England. &c.

## An Act,

Setting forth General Priveledges.

**Be it Declared and Enacted by the Governour, Council, and Representatives, of Their Majesties Province of the Massachusets Bay in New England, in General Court, Assembled and by the Authority of the same**, That all and every the Rights and Liberties of the People, in this present Act mentioned shall be Firmly and Strictly Holden and Observed.

That is to say,

THat no Freeman shall be taken and Imprisoned, or be Disseized of his Freehold, or Libertys, or his Free Customes, or be Outlawed, or Exiled, or in any manner Destroyed, Nor shall be Passed upon Adjudged or Condemned, but by the Lawful Judgment of his Peers or the Law of this Province.

Justice nor Right shall be neither sold denied or deferred to any Man within this Province.

No Man shall be twice Sentenced for one and the same Crime, Offence or Trespass.

No Aid, Tax, Tallage, Assesment, Custome, Loan, Benevolence, or Imposition whatsoever, shall be Laid, Assessed, Imposed or Levied on any of Their Majesties Subjects, or their Estates, on any Colour or Pretence whatsoever but by the Act and Consent of the Governour, Council and Representatives of the People, Assembled in General Court.

## Quieting of Possessions

No Man of what State or Condition soever shall be put out of his Lands or Tenements, nor be taken, nor Imprisoned, nor Disherited, nor Banished, nor any ways Destroyed, without being brought to answer by due process of Law.

All Trials shall be by the Verdict of Twelve Men, Peers or Equals, and of the Neighbourhood, and in the County or Shire where the Fact shall arise or grow; Whither the same be by Indictment, Information, or otherwise against the Person Offending, except in Cases where the Law of the Province shall otherwise provide.

In all Capital Cases there shall be a Grand Inquest who shall first present the Offence and then Twelve Men of the Neighbourhood to Try the Offender, who after his Plea to the Indictment, shall be allowed his Reasonable Challenges.

In all Cases whatsoever, Bail by sufficient Sureties, shall be Allowed and taken, Unless for Treason or Felony, plainly and especially expressed, and mentioned in the Warrant of Commitment.

Provided always that nothing herein contained shall be understood to Extend to Discharge out of Prison upon Bail, any Person taken in Execution for Debt, or otherwise Legally Sentenced by the Judgment of any of the Courts of record within this Province.

All Lands and Heritages within this Province shall be free from Year, Day, and Waste, Escheats and Forfeitures, upon the Death of Parents, or Ancestors, Natural, Casual, or Judicial, and that for ever: Except in cases of High Treason.

# An Act,

### For the Quieting of Possessions, and Setling of Titles.

**W**HEREAS for the Preventing of Contests and Law-Suits, referring to Housing and Lands, (there having been a) Neglect in many Persons, in the Infancy of these Plantations, to Observe a Legal Course and Method for the Passing and Confirmation of Sales and Alienations:

**It was Ordered and Enacted by the Late Governour and Company of the Massachusets-Bay, in the Year 1657.**

*ten years quiet Possession to give a Title.* That any Person or Persons, who either by Themselves, or by their Grantees, or Assigns; before the Law made for direction about Inheritances, Bearing Date *October* the Nineteenth, One Thousand SixHundred Fifty Two, have Possessed and Occupied as his or their own Proper Right, in Fee Simple, any Houses or Lands within this Jurisdiction, and shall so continue, whether

in

in their own Persons, their Heirs or Assigns, or by any other Person or Persons, from, by, or under them, without *Disturbance, Let, Suit, or Denial,* Legally made, by having the Claim of any Person thereto, Entred with the Recorder of the County, where such Houses or Lands ly; with the Names of the Persons so Claiming; and the Quantity and Bounds of the Lands, and Houses, Claimed; And such Claim prosecuted to Effect within the Term of Five Years next, after the Twentieth of *May,* One Thousand Six Hundred Fifty and Seven. Every such Proprietor, His or Her Heirs, and Assigns, by Virtue of such Possession, shall for ever after enjoy the same, without any Lawful Let, Suit, Disturbance, or Denial, by any after-Claim of any Person or Persons whatsoever; any Law, or Custome to the Contrary Notwithstanding.

Which before Recited Law referring to Possession, having been found by long Experience, to be of great Benefit and Service, unto Their Majesties Subjects, within this Their Province.

**It is Enacted and Ordained by the Governour, Council and Representatives in General Court Assembled, And by the Authority of the same, That the said Law be and hereby is Ratifyed and Confirmed; And to Continue and Remain in Full Force as Formerly.**

And for the further Quieting of Possessions and Setling of Titles.

**It is also Enacted and Ordained by the Authority aforesaid.**

That every Person and Persons for the Future shall have the like benefit of Possession, who by Him or Themselves, Grantees, or Assigns were Possessed of any Houses or Lands, within this Province, in His or Their own proper right; upon the First Day of this Instant Month *October*. And shall continue in such Possession for the Space of Three Years next after, without Disturbance or Action brought against them. *Three Years Quiet Possession to make a Title,*

Provided this Act shall not be understood to Barr the Title of any Infant, Feme-Covert, or Person *Non Compos Mentis*: Imprisoned, or in Captivity, who shall have the like time of Three Years next after such Imperfection Removed, to pursue their Challenge to any Houses or Lands wherein they have Interest or Title. And for all Persons beyond Sea, the Time of Seven Years, from the Date hereof, shall be allowed them to pursue their Challenge as aforesaid. *Savings*

## Building with Stone or Brick

# An Act,

### For Building with Stone or Brick in the Town of Boston, and preventing Fire.

**W**HEREAS Great Desolations and Ruines have sundry times happened by Fire, breaking out in the Town of *Boston*, principally occasioned by reason of the joyning and nearness of the Buildings, being mostly of Timber, and covered with Shingle. For the better preventing of such Accidents for the future, and Damage and Loss thereby.

**Be it Ordained and Enacted by the Governour Council, and Representatives, Convened in General Court or Assembly. And it is Enacted by the Authority of the same.**

*Buildings in Boston to be of Brick or Stone and covered with Slate.*

That henceforth no Dwelling House, Shop, Warehouse, Barn, Stable, or any other Housing of more than Eight Feet in Length, or Breadth, and Seven Feet in Height, shall be Erected and Set up in *Boston*, but of Stone or Brick, and covered with Slate or Tyle, unless in particular cases where necessity requires; being so judged and signified in writing under the Hands of the Justices, and Select-men of the said Town, or major part of both; the Governour with the Advice and Consent of the Council shall see cause to Grant Licence unto any person to build with Timber, or cover with Shingle. And if any person shall presume to Erect, or cause to be Erected, any Frame or Building contrary hereto; upon Conviction thereof, before two Justices of Peace ( *Quorum Unus* ) such Building shall be deemed a common Nusance and the Owner of such Frame or Building shall enter into a Recognizance to Demolish the same; and in Default of Entring into such Recognizance, shall be Committed to Prison, until he do cause the same to be Demolished; or else such Building shall be Demolished by Order of the Quarter Sessions of the Peace within the said County, and the Charge thereof to be Levied by Distress, and Sale of such Offenders Goods, by Warrant from the Court, of Quarter Sessions.

*Governour & Council to grant Licence to build with Timber in Case.*

*Penalty for transgressing this Act.*

**And it is further Ordered and Enacted,**

*Justices and Select-men to lay out Streets, &c.*

That in all Void and Unbuilt Places, which shall hereafter be improved for Building, or when at any time any total Consumption or Desolation shall happen in any Street or Lane within the said Town, it shall be in the power of the Justices of the Peace of said Town then in being, together with the Select Men, or the major part of both, to State and Lay out such Streets, Ways and Passages, as may be most for the Conveniency and Accommodation of the Place: As also where any Desolation has happened, to Regulate and Enlarge other narrow and crooked Lanes or Passages. AND where any particular persons shall have their Land taken away or lessened thereby; a Jury of Twelve

## Building with Stone or Brick

Twelve Men shall be appointed by two Justices of the Peace, and Sworn to Ascertain the value thereof, to be paid by the person, to whose Land the same shall be added, or by the Neighbourhood or Town, in proportion to the benefit or conveniency any shall have thereby. And every person Building as aforesaid with Brick or Stone, shall have liberty to Set half his Partition Wall in his Neighbours Ground, so that he leave Toothing in the Corners of such Walls for his Neighbour to adjoyn unto, who when he shall Build, such Neighbour adjoyning, shall pay for one half of the said Partition Wall, so far as it shall be Built against. And in case of any Difference arising, the Select men shall have power to appoint meet persons to value the same, or lay out the Line between such Neighbours. AND whereas several Houses and other Buildings have been Erected and Set up since the year 1688 contrary to the Law made by the General Court of the *Massachusetts* Colony;

*A Jury to Ascertain the Value of any Persons Land laid to any Street.*

*Party Wall to stand half in the Neighbours ground*

**It is hereby Ordained and Enacted by the Authority aforesaid,**

That every Owner of such House or Buildings so Set up, contrary to said Law, shall cause the same to be Covered with Slate or Tyle; or otherwise such Houses or Buildings shall be deemed a common Nusance, and the Owner thereof Proceeded against accordingly.

**And be it further Enacted and Declared by the Authority aforesaid,**

That when any Fire shall happen to break out either in *Boston*, or any other Town within this Province, two or three of the Chief Military or Civil Officers of the same Town, shall, or may, and hereby are Impowred to give Directions for the pulling down, or blowing up any such House or Houses that shall be by them adjudged meet to be pulled down or blown up, for the stopping and preventing the further Spreading of the same. And if it shall happen that the pulling down or blowing up any such House or Houses by the Directions aforesaid, shall be the occasion of stopping the said Fire, or that the Fire stop before it come to the same. That then all and every Owner of such House or Houses, shall Receive reasonable Satisfaction, and be paid for the same, by the rest of the Inhabitants; whose Houses shall not be Burnt; who are hereby Impowred to make such Rate or Rates, for the Raising and Levying of such Sum and Sums of Mony as shall be thought convenient by the Select-Men and Justices of said Town for that end.

*Two or 3 of the chief Military Officers to Order the pulling down or blowing up of Houses to stop Fire.*

*Where the Fire is stopt by pulling down or blowing up any House the owner to be paid.*

PROVIDED always, That if the House where the Fire shall first Begin and Break out, shall be adjudged fit to be pulled down or blown up to hinder the further spreading and increase of the same. That then the Owner of such House shall receive no manner of Satisfaction for the same. Any thing in this Act contained notwithstanding.

# An Act,

### For the Setling and Distribution of the Estates of Intestates.

WHEREAS Estates in these Plantations do consist chiefly of Lands which have been subdued and brought to Improvement, by the Industry and Labour of the Proprietors, with the Assistance of their Children, the younger Children generally having been longest and most Serviceable unto their Parents in that behalf; who have not Personal Estates to give out unto them in Portions or otherwise to Recompence their Labour.

**Be it therefore Enacted and Ordained by the Governour, Council, and Representatives, Convened in General Court or Assembly. And it is Ordained by the Authority of the same.**

*Persons Seized of Lands in fee simple may dispose of the same by will. &c.* That every person lawfully Seized of any Lands, Tenements, or Hereditaments within this Province, in his own proper right in Fee Simple, shall have power to give, and dispose, and devise, as well by his Last Will and Testament in Writing, as otherwise by any Act Executed in his Life all such Lands, Tenements and Hereditaments to and among his Children or others, as he shall think fit at his Pleasure. And if no such Disposition, Gift, or Devise be made by the Owner of any such Lands, Tenements and Hereditaments; the same shall be subject to a Division, with his Personal Estate, and be a like Distributed, according to the Rules herein after Exprest for Intestate Estates.

*Administrators to the Estate of Intestates how to be granted.* And when and so often as it shall happen, That any person dyes Intestate; Administration of such Intestates, Goods and Estate. shall be granted unto the Widow or next of Kin to the Intestate, or both, as the Judge for Probate of Wills, and granting of Administrations shall think fit, who shall thereupon take Bond with Sureties in manner as is directed by the Statute of the 22th and 23th of *Charles* the Second, and shall and may proceed to call such Administrators to account for, and touching the Goods of the Intestate; And upon due Hearing and Consideration thereof, (Debts, Funeral and just Expences of all sorts being first allowed) the said Judge shall, and hereby is fully Impowred to Order and make a just Distribution of the Surplusage, or remaining Goods and Estate as well Real as Personal in manner following: That is to say,

*Distribution of Intestate Estates.* One Third Part of the Personal Estate to the Wife of the Intestate for ever, besides her Dower or Thirds in the Houses and Lands during Life, where such Wife shall not be otherwise Endowed before Marriage, and all the Residue of the Real and Personal Estate by Equal Portions to and among his Children, and such as shall Legally Represent them; (if any of them be dead) other than such Children, who shall have any Estate by Settlement of the Intestate in

his

## Administration & Settlement of Intestate Estates  7

his life-time Equal to the others shares. Children advanced by Settlement, or Portions not equal to the others Shares, to have so much of the Surplusage as shall make the Estate of all to be Equal, except the Eldest Son then Surviving, (where there is no Issue of the First-born or of any other Elder Son) who shall have two Shares, or a double portion of the whole; & where there are no Sons, the Daughters shall Inherit as Coparceners. The Division of the Houses and Lands to be made by five sufficient Freeholders upon Oath, or any Three of them, to be Appointed and Sworn by the Judge for that end: unless where all the Parties Interested in any Estate being Legally capable to Act, shall mutually agree of a Division among themselves, and present the same in Writing under their Hands and Seals; in which case, such Agreement shall be accepted and allowed for a Settlement of such Estate, and be accounted valid in Law, being Acknowledged by the Parties Subscribing before the Judge, and put upon Record.

PROVIDED Nevertheless, That where any Estate in Houses and Lands cannot be divided among all the Children, without great prejudice to, or spoyling of the whole; being so Represented, and made to appear unto the said Judge, the Judge may order the whole unto the Eldest Son, if he accept it, or to any other of the Sons successively, upon his Refusal: He paying unto the other Children of the Deceased, their Equal, and proportionable Parts or Shares of the true value of such Houses and Lands. Upon a just Apprizement thereof, to be made by Three Sufficient Freeholders upon Oath, to be Appointed and Sworn as aforesaid, or giving good Security to pay the same in some convenient time, as the said Judge shall Limit, making reasonable allowance in the Interim, not exceeding six *per Cent. per Annum*. And if any of the Children happen to Dye, before he or she come of Age, or be Married; the Portion of such Child Deceased, shall be equally divided among the Survivors:

And in case there be no Children, nor any Legal Representatives of them, then one Moity of the Personal Estate shall be allotted to the Wife of the Intestate for ever; and one Third of the Real Estate, for Term of Life. The Residue both of the Real and Personal Estate, equally to every of the next of Kin of the Intestate, in equal degree, and those who Legally Represent them. No Representatives to be admitted among Collaterals after Brothers and Sisters Children. And if there be no Wife, all shall be Distributed among the Children, and if no Child, to the next of Kin to the Intestate in equal degree, and their Legal Representatives as aforesaid, and in no other manner whatsoever. And every one to whom any Share shall be allotted, shall give Bond with Sureties before the said Judge of Probate; if Debts afterwards be made to appear, to Refund and Pay back to the Administrator, His or Her Ratable part thereof, and of the Administrators Charges. The Widows Thirds or Dower in the Real Estate, at the Expiration of her Term to be alike Divided as aforesaid. Saving to any Person agrieved at any Order, Sentence or Decree made for the Settlement and Distribution of any Intestate Estate, their Right of Appeal unto the Governour and Council. Every Person so appealing, giving security to Prosecute the Appeal with Effect.

*Right of Appeal saved.*

8 Administration & Settlement of Intestate Estates

### Be it further Enacted by the Authority aforesaid

**Executors to cause Probate of Wills to be made in thirty days next after the Testators Death.**

That if any Executor or Executors of the Will of any Person deceased, Knowing of their being so named and Appointed, shall not within the Space of Thirty days next, after the Decease of the Testator, cause such Will to be proved, and Recorded in the Registers Office, of the same County where the Deceased Person last dwelt; or present the said Will, and declare his or their refusal of the Executorship. Every Executor so neglecting of his or her Trust and Duty in that behalf, (without just Excuse made and accepted for such delay) shall forfeit the Sum of Five Pounds per Month, from and after the Expiration of the said Thirty Days, until he or they shall cause Probate of such Will to be made, or present the same as aforesaid. Every such Forfeiture to be had and recovered by Action, or Information, in the Inferiour Court of Pleas, in the same County: And to be disposed of, one Moity thereof, to the use of the Poor of the Town, where the Deceased Person last dwelt; and the other Moity to him or them that shall Inform and Sue for the same. And upon any such refusal of the Executor, or Executors, the Judge shall commit Administration of the Estate of the Deceased, *Cum Testamento annexo* unto the Widow or next of Kin to the Deceased, and upon their refusal to one or more of the Principal Creditors, as he shall think fit.

**Penalty for Neglect.**

**Upon Refusal Administration to be committed: *cum Testamento annexo* Executors by Wrong.**

And if any person or persons shall Alienate or Imbezel any of the Goods or Chattels of any person Deceased, before he or they have taken out Letters of Administration, and Exhibited a true Inventory of all the know or Estate of the party Deceased. Every person or persons so Acting, shall stand Chargeable, and be liable to the Action of the Creditors and other persons grieved, as being Executors in their own wrong. And the Judge shall cause a Citation to be made out unto the Widow, or next of Kin; and upon their Neglect of appearance, or refusal, may Commit Administration of any such Estate, to some one or more of the Chief Creditors, if accepted by them, or others, as he shall think fit, upon their refusal.

**Bonds for Administration to the County Treasurer, to be put in Suit by the Judge.**

And whereas, according to the former practice of the Courts, Bonds for due Administration of the Estates of Intestates, were taken in the Name of the County Treasurer, and the Obligation made to him, his Successors in Said Office or Assigns; many of which are still depending

### It is Further Enacted by the Authority aforesaid.

That the Judge for Probate of Wills, and Granting of Administrations in the Countys respectively: be, and hereby are fully Impowred and Authorized, to call all such Administrators to account, and if need be, to put the said Bonds or any of them in suit, who shall be, and hereby are to be held and Esteemed the Assignees of the County Treasurer in that behalf to all Intents: Constructions and Purposes in the Law whatsoever.

An Act

For preventing of Frauds and Perjuries.  9

# An Act,

### For Prevention of Frauds and Perjuries.

FOR Prevention of many Fraudulent Practices which are commonly endeavoured to be upheld by Perjury, and Subornation of Perjury.

**Be it Enacted and Ordained by the Governour, Council and Representatives Convened in General Court, and by the Authority of the same,**

That from and after the last Day of *December* in this present Year One Thousand Six Hundred Ninety and Two. All Leases, Estates, Interests of Freehold, or Term of Years, or any uncertain Interest of, in, or, out of any Messuages, Lands, Tenements, or Hereditaments, made or created by Livery and Seisin only, or by Parole, and not put in writing and Signed by the Parties, so making or creating of the same, or their Agents thereunto Lawfully Authorized by writing, shall have the Force & Effect of Leases, or Estates at will only, & shall not either in Law or Equity be deemed or taken to have any other or greater Force or Effect; any consideration for making any such Parole Leases or Estates, or any former Law or Usage to the contrary notwithstanding. *(Parole Leases and Interest of Freehold shall have the force of Estates, at will only.)*

Except nevertheless, all Leases not exceeding the Term of Three Years from the making thereof, whereupon the Rent Reserved to the Landlord, during such Term shall amount unto two third parts at the least of the full improved value of the thing Demised. *(Except Leases not Exceeding three years, &c.)*

And moreover, That no Leases, Estates or Interests, either of Freehold, or Term of Years, or any uncertain Interest of in, to or out of any Messuages, Lands, Tenements or Hereditaments, shall at any time after the said last day of *December*, be Assigned, Granted, or Surrendred, unless it be by Deed or Note in Writing, Signed by the Party so Assigning, Granting or Surrendring the same, or their Agents thereunto lawfully Authorized by Writing, or by Act and Operation of Law. *(No Leases or states of Freehold to be granted or surrendred by word.)*

**And be it further Enacted by the Authority aforesaid.**

That from and after the said last day of *December*, no Action shall be brought whereby to Charge any Executor or Administrator upon any special Promise, to answer Damages out of his own Estate, (2) or whereby to Charge the Defendant upon any special Promise to answer for the Debt, Default or Miscarriages of another person, (3) or to charge any person upon any Agreement made upon consideration of Marriage, (4) or upon any Contract or Sale of Lands, Tenements or Hereditaments, or any Interest in, or concerning *(Promises and Agreements by Parole.)*

C 2

concerning them; (5) or upon any Agreement that is not to be performed within the space of one year from the making thereof; (6) unless the Agreement upon which such Action shall be brought, or some Memorandum or Note thereof shall be in Writing, and Signed by the Party, to be Charged therewith, or some other person thereunto by him lawfully Authorized.

## And be it further Enacted by the Authority aforesaid,

*Devises of Lands to be in Writing & attested by three or four Witnesses,*

That from and after the said last day of *December*, all Devises and Bequests of any Lands or Tenements, shall be in Writing, and Signed by the Party, so Devising the same, or by some other person in his presence, and by his express Directions, and shall be Attested and Subscribed in the presence of the said Devisor, by three or four credible Witnesses, or else shall be utterly void and of none Effect.

*How the same shall be revocable.*

And moreover, no Devise in Writing of Lands, Tenements or Hereditaments, or any Clause thereof, shall at any time after the said last day of *December*, be Revocable, otherwise than by some other Will or Codicil in Writing, or other Writing declaring the same, or by Burning, Cancelling, Tearing or Obliterating the same by the Testator himself, or in his presence, and by his Directions and Consent; (2) But all Devises and Bequests of Lands and Tenements shall remain and continue in full force, until the same be Burnt, Cancelled, Torn or Obliterated by the Testator, or his Direction in manner aforesaid, or unless the same be altered by some other Will or Codicil in Writing, or other Writing of the Devisor, Signed in the presence of three or four Witnesses, declaring the same; any former Law or Usage to the contrary Notwithstanding.

## And be it further Enacted by the Authority aforesaid,

*All Declarations or Creations of trust to be in Writing.*

That from and after the said last day of *December*, all Declarations or Creations of Trusts, or Confidences of any Lands, Tenements or Hereditaments, shall be manifested and proved by some Writing, Signed by the Party who is by Law enabled to declare such Trust, or by his Last Will in Writing, or else they shall be utterly void and of none effect.

*Trusts arising, transferred or extinguished by implication of Law excepted.*

Provided always, That where any Conveyance shall be made of any Lands or Tenements, by which a Trust or Confidence shall or may arise or result by the Implication or Construction of Law, or be Transferred or Extinguished by an Act or Operation of Law, then, and in every such case, such Trust or Confidence shall be of the like Force and Effect as the same would have been, if this Act had not been made; any thing herein before contained to the contrary notwithstanding.

## And be it further Enacted,

*Assignments of trust shall be in writing*

That all Grants and Assignments of any Trust or Confidence, shall likewise be in Writing, Signed by the Party, Granting or Assigning the same by such Last Will or Devise, or else shall be utterly void and of none Effect.

and

### And be it further Enacted by the Authority aforesaid.

*Contract for Sale of Goods for Ten Pounds, or more.*

That from and after the said last day of *December*, No Contract for the Sale of any Goods, Wares and Merchandizes, for the price of Ten Pounds, or upwards, shall be allowed to be good, except the Buyer shall accept part of the Goods so Sold, and actually receive the same, or give something in Earnest to bind the Bargain, or in part of payment, or that some Note or Memorandum in Writing of the said Bargain, be Made and Signed by the Parties to be Charged by such Contract, or their Agents thereunto lawfully Authorized.

And for prevention of Fraudulent Practices, in Setting up Nuncupative Wills, which have been the occasion of much Perjury.

*Nuncupative Wills.*

### Be it Enacted by the Authority aforesaid,

That from and after the aforesaid last day of *December*, No Nuncupative Will shall be good, whereby the Estate thereby Bequeathed, shall exceed the value of Thirty Pounds, that is not proved by the Oaths of Three Witnesses ( at the least ) that were present at the making thereof, nor unless it be proved that the Testator at the time of pronouncing the same, did bid the persons present, or some of them, bear witness, that such was his Will, or to that effect ; nor unless such Nuncupative Will were made in the time of the last Sickness of the Deceased, and in the House of his or their Habitation or Dwelling, or where he or she hath been Resident, for the space of ten days, or more, next before the making of such Will, except where such person was surprized or taken Sick, being from his own home, and Dyed before he returned to the place of his or her Dwelling.

### And be it further Enacted,

That after six months passed after the speaking of the pretended Testamentary Words, no Testimony shall be received to prove any Will Nuncupative, except the said Testimony, or the Substance thereof were committed to writing within six days, after the making of the said Will.

### And be it further Enacted,

That no Letters Testamentary, or probate of any Nuncupative Will, shall pass the Seal of any Court, till fourteen days at the least after the Decease of the Testator, be fully expired, nor shall any Nuncupative will be at any time received to be proved, unless process have first issued to call in the Widow, or next of Kindred to the Deceased, to the end they may contest the same, if they please.

*Probate of Nuncupative Wills.*

### And be it further Enacted,

That no Will in writing, concerning any Goods or Chattels, or Personal Estate, shall be Repealed ; nor shall any Clause, Devise or Bequest therein, be altered or changed by any Words, or Will, by word of mouth only, except the same be in the Life of the Testator, committed to Writing, and Read to the Testator, and allowed by him, and proved to be so done by Three Witnesses at the least.

D
Provided

**Souldiers & Mariners Wills excepted.**  Provided always, That notwithstanding this Act, any Souldier being in actual Military Service, or any Mariner or Seaman being at Sea, may dispose of his Moveables, Wages, and Personal Estate, as he or they might have done before the making of this Act.

# An Act,

## For the Equal Distribution of Insolvent Estates.

**B**E it Enacted and Ordained by the Governour, Council, and Representatives, Convened in General Court or Assembly. And it is Enacted and Ordained by the Authority of the same.

**Insolvent Estates to be proportioned to the Creditors.**

**The Judge of Probate to appoint Commissioners.**

**Publick notice to be given in the County where the Deceased last dwelt, in the two next Counties.**

**Six or twelve Months to be allowed for bringing in of claims**

**The Commissioners to make Report**

**The Widows Dower saved.**

That where the Estate of any person Deceased, shall be Insolvent or insufficient to pay all Just Debts, which the Deceased owed, the same shall be set forth, and distributed to and among all the Creditors in proportion unto the Sums to them respectively owing, so far as the said Estate will Extend. For which end the Executors or Administrators appointed to any such Insolvent Estate before payment to any be made, shall Represent the Condition and Circumstances thereof unto the Judge for Probate of Wills, and granting Administrations, within the same County in which such Deceased person last dwelt, and the said Judge shall Nominate and Appoint two or more fitt persons to be Commissioners, with full power to receive, and Examine all Claims of the several Creditors, and how they are made out. And such Commissioners shall cause the time and place for their Meeting to attend the Creditors, to be Published and made known, by posting up the same in some Publick places in the Shire Town of that County where such Deceased person last dwelt, and of the two next adjoyning Countys: And Six or Twelve Moneths time ( as the Circumstances of any Estate may require ) shall be allowed by the Judge unto the Creditors for the bringing in of their Claims, and proving their Debts, at the end of which Limited time, such Commissioners shall make their report, and present a List of all the Claims unto the said Judge, who shall Order them meet Recompence out of the Estate for their Care and Labour in that affair ; as also shall Order the Sickness and necessary Funeral Expences of the Deceased, to be first paid, and the Residue and Remainder of the Estate to be paid and distributed to and among the Creditors, that shall have made out their Claims, in due proportion to the Sums to them respectively Owing, according as the Estate will bear ; saving unto the Widow ( if any be ) her right of

Dower

# For Regulating the Aſſize of Cask &c.

Dower according to Law in Houſes and Lands of the Deceaſed, the Widows Dower at the Expiration of her Term, to be diſtributed among the Creditors in a like Proportion. And no Proceſs in Law ſhall be allowed againſt the Executors or Adminiſtrators of any ſuch Inſolvent Eſtate ſo long as the ſame ſhall be depending as aforeſaid. And whatſoever Creditor ſhall not Enter and make out his or her Claim with ſuch Commiſſioners before the full Expiration of the Limited time, ſuch Perſon ſhall for ever after be debarred of his or her Debt, unleſs he or ſhe can find ſome further Eſtate of the Deceaſed, not before Diſcovered, and put into the Inventory.

**Further it is Enacted and Ordained, by the Authority aforeſaid,**

That Every Judge for Probate of Wills, and granting Adminiſtrations, within the Reſpective Countys, be, and hereby are fully Authorized, and Impowred, to Require, and Adminiſter an Oath, to any Perſon or Perſons, Suſpected to have Concealed, Imbezelled, or Conveyed away, any of the Money, Goods, or Chattels, left by any Perſon, or Perſons deceaſed for the Diſcovery of the ſame.

*The Judge of Probate Impowred to Adminiſter an Oath to perſons ſuſpected of Concealment.*

# An Act,

## For Regulating the Aſſize of Cask, and preventing Deceit in Packing of Fiſh, Beef, and Pork, for Sale.

**Be it Ordained and Enacted by the Governour Council and Repreſentatives in General Court aſſembled, and by the Authority of the ſame.**

That from and after the Firſt Day of *December* next, all Sorts and Kinds of Thight Cask uſed for any Liquor, Fiſh, Beef, Pork, or any other Commodities, within this Their Majeſties Province, ſhall be of *London* Aſſize. That is to ſay, Butts to contain One Hundred and Twenty Six Gallons. Puncheons Eighty Four Gallons. Hogſheads Sixty Three Gallons. Tearſes Forty Two Gallons. Barrels Thirty one Gallons and a Half. And made of ſound well ſeaſoned Timber, and free of Sap. And that fit Perſons, be appointed, from time to time, in all places needful, to View and Gage all ſuch Cask ; and ſuch as ſhall be found of due Aſſize, ſhall be Marked with the Gagers Mark, who ſhall have for his Pains, Four pence *Per* Tunn, and every Cooper ſhall ſet his diſtinct Brand-Mark on his own Cask ; on Penalty of Forty Shillings.

*Aſſize of Cask. Gagers to be appointed Cask to be markt by the Gager, & his Fee Every Cooper to have a diſtinct brand And Mark.*

D e

**For Regulating the Assize of Cask &c.**

*Defective Cask to be Forfeited.*

And whosoever shall put to Sale any New Cask, being defective, either in Workmanship, Timber, or Assize, as aforesaid; upon Proof thereof, made before one Justice of the Peace, he shall Forfeit such Cask, and be Fined the Sum of Ten Shillings.

**And be it further Enacted by the Authority aforesaid.**

*Quarter Sessions to appoint gagers and packers, and Swear them.*

That the Justices of the Peace, at their First General Quarter Sessions, to be holden in each Respective County, within this Province; shall Yearly, in every Town needful thereof, Choose and Appoint a fit Person or Persons, to be Gagers and Packers, and them to Swear to the Due Execution of their Office;

*Penalty of Refusal*

which if any Person so appointed, shall refuse, he shall pay the Sum of Forty Shillings, and another shall be Chosen and Appointed in his stead. And every Gager and Packer shall take care that all Cask in which he Packs Beef, Pork, Mackarel, Fish, or other Goods committed to his care, be of true and full Assize, and that he Pack the same in no other Cask whatsoever, on penalty of Ten Shillings for every Cask by him Packed, that is or shall be defective in that Respect. And if any of the beforementioned Provisions shall be packed into Half Barrels, or Tirkins, the same shall be made in Proportion to the Assize aforesaid; and be marked by the Packer.

*Ten Shillings penalty for packing in any Cask under Assize.*

And for the preventing of Fraud and Deceit in the Packing of Pickled Fish; Beef and Pork to be put to Sale.

**Be it further enacted by the authority aforesaid.**

*The whole half & quarter of meat to be put up and not the best left out Fish to be all of one kind*

That in every Town, where such Goods are Packt up for Sale, the Gager or Packer of such Town, or of the Town wherein they are put to Sale, or Shipped, shall see that it be well and orderly Performed, (that is to say) Beef and Pork, the whole Half and Quarter, and so proportionably, that the best be not left out, and so Fish and Mackarel, that they be Packed all of one kind; & that all Casks so packed be full, and the Fish found and well Seasoned, Setting his Seal on all Cask so packed, and he shall recieve of the owners for so Packing, and Sealing, Four Shillings *Per* Ton. And if any such provisions, be put to Sale, or Shipped off without the Packers mark, they shall be Forfeited.

*Four Shilper Ton for packing and Sealing.*

**And it is further Enacted.**

*Fish, and Flesh for Transportation to be Searched and Repacked by the Packer.*

That all sorts of green or pickled Fish, Sturgeon, or Flesh that shall be put up for Transportation to a Forreign Market, shall be Searched, Surveyed and approved by a Sworn Packer, who shall take strict care that the same be put up in Tight Cask of FullGage, Salted with Suitable Salt. And such as shall be so saved, and for its Condition found Merchantable, and full, the Packer shall Seal with such Brand-Mark, as shall be assigned to the Town, and such other Cut-Mark added, as may denote the Sort of Provision, and time when Packed. And all such other Provision as the Packer shall find wholsome and useful, tho' for it's Quality it be not Merchantable; he shall cause to be well Packed, Salted Filled, and Sealed with the Letter R. and such other Letters as may signifie the Town, Specie, and time of Packing. And if any Master of a Ship, or other Vessel, or any Officers, or Marriners, belonging thereto shall recieve such Provisions not marked, and Sealed, as aforesaid, aboard any of their Ships or Vessels, he or they who shall offend therein, shall Forfeit Double

*Penalty on Masters and Mariners taking any Provisions a Board, Unsealed*

## For Regulating the Assize of Cask &c. 15

Double the value of all such Provisions; and he that owns the Provisions, shall Forfeit the same. And if any Cooper, or other person shall Shift any Fish or Flesh, either on Board, or on Shore, after the same hath been so Sealed and Marked by the Packer, and Ship and Export the same, the Packer having not allowed thereof, and anew Sealed and Marked the Cask where into such Provisions are Shifted: All Persons Acting, Ordering, or Assisting therein, shall be Set in the Pillory, not exceeding one hour, and shall likewise pay Double Damages to persons wronged thereby. *Penalty for Shifting of Provisions after Sealing.*

### And it is further Enacted by the Authority aforesaid

That where any such Provisions have lain above three months under the Packers Mark, betwixt the Months of *May* and *October*, they shall again, upon Exportation or Sale, be viewed or searched by the Packer, (that is to say) so many of them as may probably discover the Condition of the whole; and if any be decayed or deceitfully dealt with, the Packer shall Cull and Repack the same, so as to distinguish, and mark them for Merchantable, or refuse, according to their Condition. And if those who Ship or Export any such Provision, shall neglect or refuse such second Search or Survey, the Packer is hereby Ordered and Impowred to deface his former Mark, and for so doing, shall be paid as if he had Repackt the same. And if the Owner Refuse to satisfie the Packer, such Packer shall have Redress on Complaint to any Justice of the Peace; who is hereby Impowred to compel the payment thereof by Distress. *Provisions that have lain three months packt in the Summer, to be Reviewed.*

### And it is further Enacted by the Authority aforesaid,

That all Tarr that shall be Exposed to Sale, within this Province, shall be in Barrels, half Barrels, and thirds of a Barrel of the Measure and Assize following; (that is to say) the Barrel to contain Thirty Gallons, the half Barrel and third of a Barrel, of the same Gage proportionably, and in no other Cask whatsoever. And all Cask to be made of the same Assize, and Branded by the Cooper as aforesaid, on pain of Forfeiture of all such Cask as are not of due Assize. And if any Tarr shall be exposed to Sale in any Cask not branded as aforesaid, the same shall be likewise Forfeited. *Assize of Cask for Tarr.*

### And further it is Enacted by the Authority aforesaid,

That all Fines, Penalties and Forfeitures arising by force and virtue of this Act, shall be the one half to Their Majesties, towards the Support of the Government of this Province; and the other half to him or them that shall Inform and Sue for the same in any of their Majesties Courts of Record within this Province. *One half of the Fines & Forfeitures to be unto Their Majesties, and the other half to the Informer.*

### Be it further Enacted by the Authority aforesaid,

That there be a Measurer of Salt, and Culler of Fish in every Sea-port Town *Measurer of Salt and Culler of Fish*

E

Town within this Province, to be appointed as aforesaid, who being likewise Sworn for the faithful Discharge of that Office, shall Cull all Merchantable Fish, and Measure all Salt that shall be Imported and Sold out of any Ship or other Vessel, and shall have three-half-pence for every Hogshead of Salt by him so Measured, to be paid, the one half by the Buyer, the other half by the Seller. And one penny *per* Quintal, for every Quintal of Merchantable Fish by him Culled, to be paid, one half by the Buyer, and the other half by the Seller.

# An Act,

## For the Punishing of Criminal Offenders.

**BE it Enacted and Ordained by the Governour, Council and Representatives in General Court Assembled, and by the Authority of the same,**

*Cursing and Swearing*
That if any person or persons shall prophanely Sware or Curse in the hearing of any Justice of the Peace, or shall be thereof Convicted by the Oathes of two Witnesses, or Confession of the party, before any Justice or Justices of the Peace; Every such Offender shall forfeit and pay unto the use of the Poor of the Town, where the offence shall be Committed, the Sum of Five Shillings. And if the Offender be not able to pay the said Sum, then to be set in the Stocks, not Exceeding two Hours. And if any person shall utter more profane Oaths or Curses at the same time, and in hearing of the same person or persons, he shall forfeit and pay to the use aforesaid the Sum of Twelve pence for every Oath or Curse after the first; or be set in the Stocks three Hours. Provided that Every

*Presumption.* offence against this Law shall be Complained of and proved as aforesaid within Thirty dayes next after the offence Committed.

**Further it is Enacted by the Authority aforesaid.**

*Drunkenness.* That every person, Convicted of Drunkenness by view of any Justice of Peace; Confession of the party; or Oaths of Two Witnesses; Such Person so Convicted, shall forfeit and pay unto the use of the Poor of the Town where Such Offence is Committed, the Sum of Five Shillings for every such Offence: And if the Offender be unable to Pay the said Sum;

to

# For the Punishing of Criminal Offenders

to be set in the Stocks, not exceeding Three Hours; at the Discretion of the Justice or Justices, before whom the Conviction shall be. And upon a second Conviction of Drunkenness, every such Offender, over and above the penalty aforesaid, shall be Bound with two Sureties in the Sum of Ten Pounds with Condition for the good Behaviour: And for want of such Sureties, shall be sent to the Common Goal, until he find the same. PROVIDED, That no Person shall be Impeached or Molested for any Offence against this Act, unless he shall be thereof Presented, Indicted or Convicted within six Months after the Offence Committed. And the Justice or Justices before whom Conviction of any of the aforesaid Offences shall be, are hereby Impowred and Authorized to Restrain or Commit the Offender, until the Fine Imposed for such Offence, be satisfied; or to cause the same to be Levied by Distress, and Sale of the Offenders Goods, by Warrant directed to the Constable; returning the Over-plus (if any be,) all such Fines to be Levied within one Week next after such Conviction, and Delivered to the Select-Men, or Overseers of the Poor, for the Use of the Poor as aforesaid.

***It is further Enacted and Ordained, by the Authority aforesaid,***

That whosoever shall Steal or Purloin any Money, Goods or Chattels, being thereof Convicted, by Confession, or Sufficient Witness upon Oath: Every such Offender, shall Forfeit treble the value of the Money, Goods or Chattels so Stollen or Purloined, unto the Owner or Owners thereof; And be further punished, by Fine or Whipping; at the discretion of the Court or Justices, that have Cognizance of such Offence; not exceeding the Sum of Five Pounds, or Twenty Stripes. And if any such Offender be unable to make Restitution, or Pay such Threefold Damages; such Offender shall be Enjoyned to make Satisfaction by Service: And the Prosecutor shall be, and hereby is Impowred to dispose of said Offender in Service to any of Their Majesties Subjects, for such Term as shall be Assigned by the Court, or Justices before whom the Prosecution was. And every Justice of Peace in the County where such Offence is Committed, or where the Thief shall be Apprehended, is hereby Authorized to Hear and Determine all Offences against this Law. PROVIDED, That the Damage exceed not the Sum of Forty Shillings. *Theft.*

And if any Person shall Commit Burglary, by Breaking up any Dwelling-House, Warehouse, Shop, Mill, Malt-house, Barn, Out-House, or any Ship or other Vessel, lying within the Body of the County, or shall Rob any Person in the Field or High-ways: Every Person so Offending, shall upon Conviction, be Branded on the Forehead with the Letter B. and upon a Second Conviction, shall be Set upon the Gallows for the space of one Hour, with a Rope about his Neck, and one end thereof cast over the Gallows; and be severely Whipt; not exceeding Thirty Nine Stripes: And upon a Third Conviction of the like Offence, shall Suffer the pains of Death, as being Incorrigible; and shall likewise upon the First and Second Convictions, pay treble Damages to the Party Injured; as is Provided in case of Theft. *Burglary.*

and

### And it is further Enacted by the Authority aforesaid.

*Fornication.*

That if any Man Commit Fornication with any single Woman; upon due Conviction thereof, they shall be Fined unto Their Majesties, not exceeding the Sum of Five Pounds; or be Corporally Punished by Whipping, not exceeding Ten Stripes a piece; at the Discretion of the Sessions of the Peace, who shall have Cognizance of the Offence. And he that is Accused by any Woman, to be the Father of a Bastard Child, Begotten of her Body; she continuing Constant in such Accusation, being Examined upon Oath, and put upon the Discovery of the Truth in the Time of her Travail; shall be adjudged the Reputed Father of such Child, Notwithstanding his Denial; and stand charged with the Maintenance thereof, with the Assistance of the Mother; as the Justices in the Quarter Sessions shall Order; and give Security to perform the said Order; and to save the Town or Place where such Child is Born, free from Charge for it's Maintenance; and may be Committed to Prison, until he find Sureties for the same, unless the Plea's and Proofs made and produced on the behalf of the Man accused, and other Circumstances be such as the Justices shall see reason to Judg him Innocent, and acquit him thereof, and otherwise dispose of the Child. And every Justice of the Peace upon his Discretion, may Bind to the Next Quarter Sessions, him that is Charged, or Suspected, to have Begotten a Bastard Child: and if the Woman be not then Delivered, the Sessions may Order the Continuance, or Renewal of his Bond, that he may be forth-coming when the Child is Born.

### Further it is Enacted by the Authority aforesaid.

*Power of the Justice of Peace.*

That every Justice of the Peace in the County where the Offence is Committed, may cause to be Staid and Arrested all Affrayers, Rioters, Disturbers, or Breakers of the Peace, and such as shall Ride, or go Armed offensively before any of Their Majesties Justices, or other Their Officers or Ministers doing their Office, or elsewhere, by Night or by Day, in Fear or Affray of Their Majesties Liege People; and such others as shall Utter any Menaces or Threatning Speeches: And upon view of such Justice or Justices, Confession of the Party, or other Legal Conviction of any such Offence, shall Commit the Offender to Prison, until he find Sureties for the Peace and good Behaviour; and Seiz and Take away his Armour or Weapons; and shall cause them to be Apprized and Answered to the King as Forfeited: And may further punish the Breach of the Peace, in any person that shall Smite or Strike another, by Fine to the King, not exceeding Twenty Shillings; and Require Bond with Sureties for the Peace; or Bind the Offender over to answer it at the next Sessions of the Peace, as the Nature or Circumstance of the Offence may be; and may make Enquiry of forcible Entry and Detainer, and cause the same to be Removed; and make out Hue and Crys after Runaway Servants, Thiefs, and other Criminals.

*Breach of the Peace.*
*Forcible Entry & detainer*

AND

## For the Punishing of Criminal Offenders.

### And it is further Enacted by the authority aforesaid.

That if any person or persons of the Age of Discretion (which is accounted Fourteen Years, or Upwards) shall wittingly and willingly Make or Publish any Lye or Libel, tending to the Defamation or Damage of any particular person or persons; Make or Spread any False News, or Reports with intent to abuse and deceive others: Every such person or persons offending in any of the particulars before-mentioned, and being duly Convicted thereof, before one or more Justices of the Peace, shall be Fined according to the degree of such Offence; not exceeding the Sum of Twenty Shillings for the First Conviction; and find Sureties for the good Behaviour. And if the Party be unable to pay the said Fine, then to be Set in the Stocks, not exceeding Three Hours; or be corporally punished by Whipping, at the discretion of the Justice or Justices, before whom the Conviction shall be; according as the Circumstances or Nature of the Offence shall be. And the said Justice or Justices may Restrain and Commit the Offender, until he pay the said Fine, and find Sureties for the good Behaviour; Or may cause the Fine to be Levied by Distress and Sale of the Offenders Goods. And the Party or Parties grieved or injured by reason of any of the Offences aforesaid; shall or may take his or their Suit against any such Offender or Offenders in any Court of Record.

*Lying and Libelling.*

### It is further Enacted by the Authority aforesaid,

That if any person or persons upon his or their own Head or Imagination, or by false Conspiracy and Fraud with others, shall wittingly, subtilly, and falsely Forge or Make; or subtilly Cause, or wittingly Assent to be Forged or Made any False Deed, Conveyance, or Writing Sealed, or the Will of any person or persons in Writing, to the intent that the State of Freehold or Inheritance, Right, Title, or Interest of any person or Persons of, in, or to any Lands, Tenements or Hereditaments shall or may be Molested, Troubled, Defeated, Recovered or Charged; or shall as is aforesaid, Forge, Make, or Cause, or Assent to be Made, or Forged, any Obligation, or Bill Obligatory, Letter of Attourney, or any Acquittance, Release, or other Discharge of any Debt, Accompt, Action, Suit, Demand, or other thing personal; Or if any person or persons shall Pronounce, Publish, or Shew forth in Evidence, any such False and Forged Deed, Conveyance, Writing, Obligation, Bill Obligatory, Letter of Attorney, Acquittance, Release or Discharge, as true, Knowing the same to be False and Forged as is aforesaid, to the Intent above Remembred; and shall be thereof Convicted, either upon Action or Actions of Forger of False Deeds to be Founded upon this Act at the Suit of the Party grieved, or otherwise according to the Order and due Course of Law, or upon Bill or Information. That then every such Offender shall pay unto the Party grieved his double Costs and Damages, to be found and Assessed in such Court where the said Conviction shall be; and also shall be Set upon the Pillory in some Market

*Forgery.*

## For the Punishing of Criminal Offenders

Market Town, or other open Place, and there to have one of his Ears cut off, and also shall have and suffer Imprisonment by the space of one whole Year, without Bail or Mainprize. And the Party or Parties grieved by reason of any of the Offences aforesaid, may take his or their Suit against any such Offender or Offenders, in any Court of Record; where no Essoign, Injunction or Protection shall be allowed the Party Defendant.

Provided always, and it is Enacted by the Authority aforesaid, That this Act, or any thing therein contained, shall not extend to charge any Judge of Probate, or Register, with any the Offences aforesaid, for putting their Seal of Office to any Will to be Exhibited unto them, not knowing the same to be False or Forged, for Writing of the said Will or Probate of the same. Nor to any other Person or Persons that shall shew forth or give in Evidence any False or Forged Writing for true or good, being not party or privy to the Forging of the same, nor knowing the same to be False or Forged, any thing in this Act to the contrary notwithstanding.

### And it is further Enacted and Ordained by the authority aforesaid.

*Wilful Perjury.*

If Any Person or Persons; either by the Subornation, unlawful procurement, reward, Sinister perswasion, or means of any other; or by their own Act, Consent, or Agrement, shall Wilfully and corruptly; commit any manner of Wilful Perjury, by his or their Deposition in any Court of Record, or being Examined *Ad Perpetuam rei memoriam*, That then every Person and Persons so Offending, and being thereof duely Convict, or Attainted By Law, shall for his or their Offence, Loose and Forfeit Twenty Pounds; the one Moiety thereof, unto their Majesties, and the other Moity to such Person or Persons as shall be Grieved, hindred or Molested by reason of any such Offence, that shall Sue for the same by Action of Debt, Bill, Plaint, Information, or otherwise, in any Court of Record; in the which no Wager of Law, Essoign, Protection, or Injunction to be allowed: And also to have Imprisonment by the Space of Six Months, without Bail, or Mainprise. And the Oath of such Person or Persons so Offending, not to be received in any Court of Record, until such time as the Judgment given against the said Person or Persons, shall be reversed by attaint or otherwise; and upon every such reversal, the Parties agrieved to recover his or their Damages against all and every such Person & Persons, as did procure the said Judgment so reversed, to be given against them or any of them, by Action or Actions, upon his or their Case or Cases; according to the Course of the Common Law.

AND if it happen, the Said Offender or Offenders, so Offending, not to have any Goods or Chattels, to the Value of Twenty Pounds, that then He or they be Set on the Pillory by the space of one whole hour, in some Market Town where the Offence was Committed, or next adjoyning to the place, where the Offence was Committed; and to have both his Ears Nailed; and from thence forth to be discredited and disabled for ever to be sworn in any Court of Record, until such Time as the Judgment shall be reversed.

AND all and every person and persons who shall unlawfully and corruptly

## Capital Crimes. 21

ly procure any Witness or Witnesses, by Letters, Rewards, Promises, or by any other Sinister and unlawful Labour or Means whatsoever; to Commit any wilful and corrupt Perjury, in any Matter or Cause whatsoever Depending, or that shall Depend in Suit and Variance, by any Writ, Action, Bill, Complaint, or Information in any Court of Record; or to Testifie *in perpetuam rei memoriam*: Every such Offender, being thereof duely Convict, or Attainted by Law, shall for his or their Offence be proceeded against, and suffer the like Pains, Penalties, Forfeitures, and Disability in all respects as above-mentioned.

**And it is further Enacted by the authority aforesaid,**

That all the aforesaid Forfeitures and Sums of Money arising for any Offence Mentioned in this Act, and every Branch thereof, and not otherwise disposed of; shall be unto Their Majesties, for and towards the Support of the Government of this Province, and the Incident Charges thereof.

# An Act,

### For the Punishing of Capital Offenders.

**Be it Ordained and Enacted by the Governour Council and Representatives in General Court assembled. And by the authority of the same.**

That all and every of the Crimes and Offences in this present Act hereafter mentioned be and hereby are declared to be Felony.

And every Person and Persons Committing any of the said Crimes or Offences, being thereof Legally Convicted, shall be Adjudged to Suffer the Pains of Death.

*Idolatry.*

IF any Man shall have or Worship any other god, but the TRUE GOD. he shall be put to death.

If

**Witchcraft**  If any Man or Woman be a WITCH; that is, hath or confulteth with a Familiar Spirit, they fhall be put to death.

**Blafphemy**  If any perfon fhall prefume to Blafpheme the Holy Name of GOD, FATHER, SON, or HOLY GHOST, either by wilful or obftinate denying the True God or His Creation, or government of the World, or fhall Curfe God in like manner, or Reproach the Holy Religion of God, as if it were but a Politick Device to keep Ignorant people in Awe, or fhall utter any other kind of Blafphemy of the like nature or degree; he fhall be put to death.

**High Treafon**  If any perfon or perfons fhall compafs or imagine the Death of Our Soveraign Lord the King or of Our Lady the Queen, or fhall Levy War againft Our faid Lord and Lady the King and Queen, or adhere unto Their Enemies, giving to them aid and comfort, and thereof be attainted or convicted of open Deed by their Peers upon the Teftimony and Depofition of Two lawful and credible Witneffes on Oath, brought before the Offender Face to Face, at the time of his Arraignment; or Voluntary confeffion of the Party Arraigned: Then every fuch perfon and perfons fo as aforefaid Offending fhall be deemed, declared

red, and adjudged to be Traitors, and shall suffer the Pains of death, and also Lose and Forfeit as in cases of High-Treason.

If any person shall commit Wilful-Murder upon premeditated Malice, Hatred, Cruelty, or sudden Heat of Anger: Every such person shall be put to death. *Murder*

If any person shall Slay another through Guile, either by Poysoning, or other Devillish Practice; every such person, their Aiders, Abettors, Procurors, and Councellors, shall suffer death, as in case of Wilful-Murder. *Poysoning*

If any Woman be delivered of any Issue of her body, Male or Female, which if it were born alive, should by Law be a Bastard; And that she endeavour privately, either by Drowning, or secret Burying thereof, or any other way; either by her self, or the procuring of others, so to conceal the death thereof, that it may not come to light, whether it were Born alive or not, but be concealed. In every such case the Mother so Offending, shall suffer death as in case of Murder; Except such Mother can make proof by one Witness at the least, that the Child whose death was by her so intended to be concealed, was born dead. *Concealment of the Death of a Bastard Child, punisht as in case of Murder.*

If any Man lieth with MANKIND, as he lieth with a Woman, they both shall be put to death. *Sodomy.*

G    If

## Capital Crimes

**Bestiality.** If any Man or Woman have carnal Copulation with any BEAST, or Bruit-Creature, they shall be put to death, and the Beast shall be slain and burned.

**Incest**
*Levit.* 20.
11,12. &c.
If any Persons commit Incest in any of the particular instances, made capital by the Law of God, they shall be put to Death.

**Rape** If a Man shall Ravish any Woman committing carnal copulation with her by force, against her will, he shall be put to death.

If any Man shall unlawfully and carnally know and abuse any Woman child, under the age of Ten Years, every such unlawful and carnal knowledge shall be Felony: And the Offender thereof, being duly convict shall suffer as a Felon.

**Burning** If any Person of the Age of Sixteen Years, and upwards, shall Wittingly Willingly and Feloniously Burn or cause to be Burned any Dwelling House, Meeting-House, Store-house, or Ship, or shall in like manner set on Fire any Out-house, Barn, Stable, Stack of Hay, Corn or Wood; Whereby any Dwelling-house, Meeting-house Store-house, or Ship, shall happen to be Burned: Every such Offender shall be put to death.

**Piracy** If any shall Piratically and Feloniously Seiz any Ship or other Vessel, whether in the Harbour,

bour, or on the High Seas; Or shall Rise up in Rebellion against the Master, Officer, Merchant or Owner of any such Ship, or other Vessel and Goods, and Dispoil and Dispossess them thereof and Exclude the right Owners or those betrusted on their behalf, Every such Offender together with their Complices, being Legally Convicted thereof, shall be put to death.

Provided always that any of such Company (who through fear or force have been deemed to comply with such wicked Action) shall upon their first Arrival in any Port or Harbour speedily repair to some Justice of the Peace and make Discovery of such Piracy, they shall not be liable to the aforesaid Penalty of Death.

. An Act

# An Act,

For the Suppressing of Unlicensed Houses, and the due Regulation of such as are, or shall be Licensed.

**None to keep a house of common Enterteinment, or Sell strong Drink publickly or privately without Licence on penalty of forty shillings.**

**One half to the Informer and the other to the use of the poor.**

**Upon second conviction to give bond for the good behaviour.**

**Licences to be renewed yearly & bond given**

**Justices may grant License without Certificate of the Select-men upon notice given.**

BE it Ordained and Enacted by the Governour, Council and Representatives Convened in General Court, and by the Authority of the same.

That no person or persons whatsoever (other than such as upon producing Certificate from the Select-men of the Town where they dwell, or who shall be otherwise thought fit by the Justices themselves, shall be Licensed by the said Justices in Quarter Sessions) may presume to be a common Victualler, Inn-holder, Taverner, or Seller of Wine, Beer, Ale, Cyder or strong Liquors by Retail. Nor shall any presume without such Licence, to Sell Wine or Strong Liquors privately by a less Quantity than a Quarter Cask, and that delivered and carried away all at one time: On pain of Forfeiting the Sum of Forty Shillings for every such Offence upon due Conviction thereof; One half thereof to the Informer, and the other half to the use of the Poor of the Town where such Offence is committed. And upon a Second Conviction, besides the Forfeiture of Forty Shillings as aforesaid, shall Enter into Recognizance with one or more Sureties for the good Behaviour, especially not to Transgress the Law in that Respect.

**Be it further Enacted by the Authority aforesaid,**

That all Licences be Renewed yearly, and Bond given for the due Observance of the same, and of the Laws, and that the Person Licensed, shall use his Licence in such House as shall be therein named, and no other.

And if the Justices in Quarter Sessions shall think fit to Licence any person or persons not presenting a Certificate as aforesaid from the Select-men, the Clerk of the Sessions, before granting Licence to any such, shall signifie the name and desire of every such person unto the Select-men of the Town where such person dwells, one month before-hand, that so they may have opportunity and liberty to offer their Objections against it, if any shall be.

And forasmuch as the ancient, and principal use of Inns, Taverns, Ale-Houses, Victualling-Houses, and other Houses for common Entertainment is for the Receipt, Relief and Lodging of Travellers and Strangers, and the Refreshment of persons upon lawful Business; or for the necessary supply of the wants of such poor persons as are not able by greater Quantities to make

make their provision of Victuals, and are not intended for Entertainment and Harbouring of Lewd or Idle People to spend or consume their Money or Time there: Therefore to prevent the Mischiefs and great Disorders happening daily by the abuse of such Houses:

**It is further Enacted by the Authority aforesaid,**

That no Taverner, Inn-keeper, Ale-house-keeper or Victualler, shall have or keep in or about their Houses, Out-houses, Yards, Backsides, Gardens or Places to them belonging, any Dice, Cards, Tables, Bowls, Shuffleboard, Billiards, Coyts, Cales, Logats, or any other Implements used in Gaming; nor shall suffer any person or persons Resorting unto any of their Houses, to Use or Exercise any of the said Games, or any other unlawful Game or Sport within their said Houses, or any of the Dependences as aforesaid, or Places to them belonging; On pain of Forfeiting the Sum of Forty Shillings for every such Offence, upon due Conviction thereof; the said Fine to be disposed of as aforesaid. And every person convicted of Playing as aforesaid in any such House or Dependences thereof, shall Forfeit the Sum of Six Shillings and Eight Pence, to be disposed of as aforesaid.

*Games and Gaming forbidden in Publick-houses, on pain of Forty Shillings.*

*Penalty on Gamesters*

**And further it is Enacted by the authority aforesaid.**

That any person duly Summoned to give in Evidence respecting the Breach of this Act, in any of the Branches thereof, (other than the party himself, his Children or Servants) that shall refuse to give in upon his Oath when so required, what he knows relating to the Premises, shall Forfeit Forty Shillings to the use of the poor of the Town as aforesaid.

*Penalty for refusing to give Evidence against persons Selling without Licence.*

**And it is further Enacted by the Authority aforesaid.**

That every Justice of the Peace in the County where he dwells, as well as the Justices in Quarter Sessions, are hereby respectively Impowred to hear and determine all Offences against this Act, and may Commit the Offender to Prison, until he pay the said Fine, and Enter into Recognizance as aforesaid for the good Behaviour; Or may cause the Fine to be Levied by Distress and Sale of the Offenders Goods, returning the Overplus, if any be.

*One Justice may hear & determine all Offences against this Act.*

## An Additional Act,

### For Impost and Excife.

**Be it Enacted by the Governour, Council and Rprefentatives in General Court affembled, And by the authority of the fame**

That there fhall be paid by the Importer, for all Wines Imported into this Province not particularly named, and mentioned in an Act Entituled, *An Act for Impoft, Excife and Tonnage of Shipping*, made at the firft Seffions of this Court, the Sum of Ten Shillings *per* Hogfhead, and fo proportionably for greater or leffer quantities. And that there be paid by thofe that Sell any of the faid Wines by Retail, the Sum of fix pence *per* Gallon Excife, and fo proportionably for greater or leffer quantities. And to be under the fame Regulation, Infpection and Forfeitures as is provided by faid Act; & the faid payments to be made unto the Commiffioners appointed for the Receiving of the Rates and Duties therein mentioned. This prefent Act to remain and continue in force only during the time fet for continuance of the Act before Recited, and no longer.

## An Act,

### For the better Obfervation and Keeping the Lords-Day.

**Be it Enacted and Ordained by the Governour, Council and Reprefentatives Convened in General Court or Affembly, and it is enacted by the Authority of the fame.**

That all and every Perfon and Perfons whatfoever, fhall on that Day carefully apply themfelves to Duties of Religion and Piety, publickly and privately; and that no Tradef-man, Artificer, Labourer, or other perfon whatfoever, fhall upon the Land or Water, Do or Exercife any Labour,

# Keeping the Lords Day

Labour, Business, or Work of their ordinary Callings; nor use any Game, Sport, Play or Recreation on the Lords-Day, or any part thereof; (Works of Necessity and Charity only excepted) upon pain that every Person so Offending shall Forfeit Five Shillings.

*Labour and Sports Prohibited on penalty of Five Shillings*

### Further it is Ordered and Declared,

That no Traveller, Drover, Horse-Courser, Waggoner, Butcher, Higler, or any their Servants, shall Travel on that Day, or any part thereof, except by some adversity they were Belated and forced to Lodge in the Woods, Wilderness, or High-ways, the night before; and in such case, to Travel no further than the next Inn or Place of Shelter, on that Day, upon the penalty of Twenty Shillings.

*Travelling prohibited on penalty of Twenty Shillings.*

### Further it is Ordered,

That no Vintner, Inn-holder, or other Person keeping any Publick-house of Entertainment, shall Entertain or Suffer any of the Inhabitants of the Respective Towns where they Dwell, or others not being Strangers or Lodgers in such Houses, to abide or remain in their Houses, Yards, Orchards or Fields Drinking, or idly spending their time on *Saturday* night after the Sun is Set, or on the Lords-Day, or the Evening following; upon the pain and penalty of Five Shillings for every person, payable by themselves respectively that shall be found so Drinking or Abiding in any such Publick House or Dependences thereof as aforesaid; and the like Sum of Five Shillings to be paid by the Keeper of such House, for every person Entertained by them.

*Publick houses not to entertain any others than Strangers & Lodgers on penalty of Five Shillings for every person.*

And for the better Execution of all and every the foregoing Orders, every Justice of the Peace within his County shall have Power and Authority to Convent before them, any person or persons, who shall offend in any of the particulars before mentioned, and upon his own view, or other legal Conviction of any such Offence, to impose the Fine and Penalty for the same, and to Restrain or Commit the Offender until it be satisfied; or to cause the same to be Levied by Distress and Sale of the Offenders Goods, returning the Over plus (if any be) and in case any such Offender be unable or refuse to satisfie such Fine, to cause him to be put in the Cage or set in the Stocks, not exceeding three hours: All Fines and Penalties accruing by this Act, to be to the benefit and relief of the Poor of such Town where the Offence is committed; and delivered into the hands of the Select-men, or Overseers of the poor for that end.

*One Justice of the Peace may hear & determin any breach of this Act.*

*Fines for breach of this Act to be to the use of the poor.*

And all Masters and Governours of Families are hereby required to take effectual care that their Children, Servants and others under their immediate Government, do not transgress in any of the foregoing particulars.

And all and every Justices of the Peace, Constables and Tything-men are required to take effectual care and endeavour that this Act in all the particulars thereof be duly observed; as also to restrain all persons from Swimming in the water, unnecessary and unseasonable walking in the Streets or Fields in the Town of *Boston,* or other places, keeping open their Shops, or following their Secular Occasions or Recreations in the Evening preceding the Lords-Day, or on any part of the said Day or Evening following.

*Justices, Constables &c. required to see that this Act be observed.*

And all persons are strictly required to be obedient to, and aiding and assisting such Justices, Constables and other Officers herein, as they will answer the contrary at their Peril.

An

# An Act,

### For Prevention of Common Nusances arising by Slaughter-Houses, Still-Houses, &c. Tallow Chandlers, and Curriers.

**BE it Ordained and Enacted by the Governour, Council and Representatives Convened in General Court or Assembly, and by the Authority of the same,**

*Slaughter-Houses, Still-Houses, &c. to be in certain places assigned, & no other.*

That the Select-Men of the Towns of *Boston, Salem* and *Charlstown* Respectively, or other Market-Towns in the Province; with two or more Justices of the Peace Dwelling in the Town, or two of the next Justices in the County, shall at or before the last day of *March*, One Thousand Six Hundred Ninety Three, Assign some certain places in each of said Towns (where it may be least offensive) for the Erecting or Setting up of Slaughter-Houses, for the Killing of all Meat; Still-Houses, & Houses for Trying of Tallow, & Currying of Leather (which Houses may be Erected of Timber, the Law referring to Building with Brick or Stone notwithstanding) And shall cause an Entry to be made in the Town-Book, of what places shall be by them so Assigned, and make known the same by Posting it up in some Publick Places of the Town. At which Houses and Places respectively, and no other, all Butchers and Slaughter-men, Distillers, Chandlers and Curriers shall Exercise and Practice their Respective Trades and Mysteries; on pain that any Butcher or Slaughter-man transgressing of this Act, by Killing of Meat in any other place, for every Conviction thereof before one or more Justices of the Peace, shall Forfeit and Pay the Sum of Twenty Shillings. And any Distiller, Chandler or Currier offending against this Act, for every Conviction thereof before Their Majesties Justices at the General Sessions of the Peace for the County, shall Forfeit and Pay the Sum of Five Pounds; one third part of said Forfeitures to be to the use of Their Majesties, for the Support of the Government of the Province, and the Incident Charges thereof; one Third to the Poor of the Town, where such Offence shall be Committed; and the other Third to him or them that shall Inform and Sue for the same.

And for preventing of Cruelty to Bruit Creatures.

*Cruelty to bruit Creatures forbidden.*

**It is further Enacted by the Authority aforesaid.**

That all Calves, Sheep or Lambs brought alive to the Market, shall be either

# Common Nusances.

either driven; or carried in Carts, Sleds, Panyers or Boats, and not otherwise; on pain of Forfeiting of all Calves, Sheep or Lambs passing towards, or brought alive to the Market, laid acrofs, or hanging by the sides of Horses, ( as has been usual ) or in any other way contrary to the true Intent of this Act: One half of all such Forfeitures to be unto the Informers, who shall Seiz and Prosecute for the same; and the other Moity to the use of the Poor of the Town, where such Seizure shall be made, to be distributed by the Select-men or Overseers of the Poor.

And all Select-men, Overseers of the Poor, Constables, Tythingmen and other Officers in any Town upon their own view, or Information of any Transgression of this Act within their respective Precincts, shall and hereby are Impowred to Seiz or cause to be Seized all Calves, Sheep or Lambs that shall be carrying or brought alive to the Market, in any other way than is before Directed. And upon due proof thereof, made before one or more Justices of the Peace, shall be Forfeited, and the same or the value thereof be disposed of as aforesaid.

And all Veal or other Meat exposed to Sale, that shall be blown up or winded, shall be alike Forfeited and Disposed of.

# An Act,

## For Affirming of former Judgments, and providing for Executions.

WHEREAS upon Tryals had in the late Courts of Judicature within the several Colonies, now by Their Majesties Royal Charter United and Incorporated into one Province, by the name of the Province of the *Massachusetts-Bay*, several Judgements were obtained, of which Execution remains to be done, and some others are depending by Appeal, according to the course and practice of the Courts then in being. To the end that there be no failure of Justice for want of a due course of Law, for the Prosecuting, Obtaining and Levying of the same.

**Be it Enacted and Ordained by the Governour, Council and Representatives Convened in General Court or Assembly, and by the Authority of the same,**

That where any Appeal, as aforesaid, is depending, having not been heard; every such Appellant shall have a Summons  from the Clerk of

I the

the Superiour Court, unto the adverse party, to be Served upon him seven days inclusive before the Courts Sitting, Requiring him to appear at the first Superiour Court, to answer the said Appeal; where the same shall be Heard and Tryed according to former Usage upon the first Evidence and no other: And the Judgement to be Affirmed or Reversed as the Case shall there be Judged upon Tryal. And if the Appellant neglect to Appear or Prosecute his Appeal, the former Judgement shall be Affirmed, and Execution Awarded accordingly.

### And it is further Enacted by the Authority aforesaid

That where Judgement has passed in any County Court, or Court of Commissioners, and Execution has not been Taken out and Levied for satisfying of the same; the Party for whom any Judgement was so given his Executors or Administrators shall have a Writ of *Scire Facias* from the Clerk of the Inferiour Court of Pleas, within the same County, in which such Judgement was obtained, unto the Adverse Party to appear before said Court, to shew cause (if any there be) why Execution should not Issue forth. And in case of Non Appearance, or that sufficient cause be not shewn to the Court, the former Judgement shall be affirmed, and Execution granted accordingly, the Costs of this Tryal to be added unto the same. Provided, that the said Writ of *Scire Facias* be Served seven days inclusive before the Courts Sitting.

### And be it further Enacted by the Authority aforesaid.

No Execution after one year expired, to be granted without a *Scire facias*.

That after one year Expired next after giving Judgement in any Court of Record within this Province, no Execution for such Judgement shall be Issued out, until a Writ of *Scire Facias* hath been Granted out of the same Court, and Served upon the Adverse Party, as is before directed, or left by the Sheriff, his Under-Sheriff or Deputy, at his Dwelling, or Place of usual and last Abode, requiring him to appear and shew cause (if any he have) why Execution ought not to be done. And upon his Non Appearance, or not shewing of sufficient cause as aforesaid; The Court shall thereupon Award Execution.

# An Act,

For the Orderly consummating of Marriages.

**B**e it Ordained and Enacted by the Governour, Council and Representatives in General Court Assembled, and by the Authority of the same,

That every Justice of the Peace within the County where he resides, and every Setled Minister in any Town, shall and are hereby respectively Impowred and Authorized to Solemnize Marriages, within their Respective Towns and Counties, betwixt Persons that may lawfully Enter into such Relation, having the consent of those whose immediate care and Government they are under, and being likewise first Published by asking their Banns at three several Publick Meetings in both the Towns where such Parties respectively Dwell; or by Posting up their Names and Intention at some publick place in each of the said Towns, fairly written, thereto stand by the space of Fourteen Days, and producing Certificate of such Publishment under the Hand of the Town Clerk or Constable of such Towns respectively. *Justices or Ministers respectively to Solemnize Marriages*

And the Fee to be paid for every Marriage, shall be Three Shillings; and for Publishment and Certificate thereof, One Shilling. *Publishment how to be made.*

*Fee for Marriage, &c.*

**And be it further Enacted**

That whoever shall presume to deface or pull down any such Publishment, posted up in Writing, before the Expiration of the time, shall be Fined to the use of the Poor of the Town, the Sum of Ten Shillings, being Convicted thereof, before one or more Justices of the Peace: And if the Party be unable to pay the said Fine, then to be Set in the Stocks one whole Hour. *Penalty for pulling down publishments*

And every Justice and Minister shall keep a particular Register of all Marriages Solemnized before any of them, and make a Return thereof at the end of each Quarter of a year unto the Clerk of the Sessions of the Peace within the same County, to be by him Registred; who is hereby Impowred thereto, and shall be paid by every such Justice and Minister, Three-Pence for each Marriage so Returned. *Marriages to be Registred.*

**And it is further Enacted by the Authority aforesaid.**

That all Controversies concerning Marriage and Divorce, shall be Heard and Determined by the Governour and Council, *Divorce*

# An Act,

### For the Setlement and Support of Ministers and School-Masters.

**Be it Ordained and Enacted by the Governour, Council and Representatives Convened in General Court or Assembly, and by the Authority of the same.**

That the Inhabitants of each Town within this Province, shall take due care from time to time, to be constantly provided of an Able, Learned, Orthodox Minister or Ministers, of good Conversation, to Dispense the Word of God to them; which Minister or Ministers shall be suitably Encouraged and sufficiently Supported and Maintained by the Inhabitants of such Town. And all Contracts, Agreements and Orders heretofore made, or that shall hereafter be made by the Inhabitants of any Town within this Province, respecting their Ministers or School-Masters, as to their Setlement or Maintainance, shall remain good and valid according to the true Intent thereof, the whole time for which they were or shall be made, in all the particulars thereof, and shall accordingly be pursued, put in Execution and Fulfilled. And where there is no Contract and Agreement made in any Town respecting the Support and Maintainance of the Ministry; or when the same happens to be Expired, and the Inhabitants of such Town shall neglect to make suitable provision therein; Upon Complaint thereof made unto the Quarter Sessions of the Peace for the County where such Town lies; the said Court of Quarter Sessions shall, and hereby are Impowred to Order a Competent Allowance unto such Minister according to the Estate & Ability of the Town: the same to be Assessed upon the Inhabitants by Warrant from the Court, directed to the Select-men, who are thereupon to proceed to make and proportion such Assesment in manner as is directed for other Publick Charges, and to cause the same to be Levied by the Constables of such Town, by Warrant under the Hands of the Select-men; or of the Town Clerk by their Order.

*Contracts & Agreements to be made good*

*Neglect of making suitable provision for Ministers to be redressed by the Quarter Sessions*

*The Court of Quarter Sessions to take care that no Town be destitute of a Minister.*

**Be it further Enacted by the authority aforesaid.**

That where any Town shall be destitute of a Minister qualified as aforesaid, and shall so continue by the space of six Months, not having taken due care for the procuring, Setling and Encouragement of such Minister, the same being made to appear upon Complaint unto Their Majesties Justices

at

## Ministers and School Masters 35

at the General Sessions of the Peace for the County, the said Court of Quarter Sessions shall, and hereby are Impowred to make an Order upon every such defective Town, speedily to provide themselves of such Minister as aforesaid, by the next Sessions at the furthest; and in case such Order be not complied with, then the said Court shall take effectual care to procure and Settle a Minister qualified as aforesaid, and Order the Charge thereof and of such Ministers Maintainance to be Levied on the Inhabitants of such Town.

### And it is further Enacted by the Authority aforesaid,

That the Respective Churches in the several Towns within this Province, shall at all times hereafter, Use, Exercise and Enjoy all their Priviledges and Freedoms respecting Divine Worship, Church-Order and Discipline, And shall be Encouraged in the peaceable and regular Profession and Practice thereof. *Churches to enjoy their Priviledges & Freedoms.*

### And further it is Enacted,

That every Minister being a person of good Conversation, Able, Learned and Orthodox, that shall be Chosen by the major part of the Inhabitants in any Town, at a Town-Meeting duly warned for that purpose, (notice thereof being given to the Inhabitants fifteen days before the time for such Meeting,) shall be the Minister of such Town; and the whole Town shall be obliged to pay towards his Settlement and Maintainance, each man his several proportion thereof. *Ministers Chosen by the major part of the Inhabitants, to be the Minister of such Town.*

### And it is further Enacted by the Authority aforesaid,

That every Town within this Province, having the Number of Fifty House-holders or upwards, shall be constantly provided of a School-Master to Teach Children and Youth to Read and Write. And where any Town or Towns have the number of One Hundred Families or Housholders, there shall also be a Grammar School set up in every such Town, and some discreet person of good Conversation well Instructed in the Tongues procured to keep such School. Every such School-Master to be suitably Encouraged and Paid by the Inhabitants. *School for Reading and Writing. Grammar School.*

And the Select-men and Inhabitants of such Towns respectively shall take effectual care and make due provision for the Settlement and Maintenance of such School-Master and Masters. *School-masters to be Supported*

And if any Town Qualified as before exprest, shall neglect the due Observance of this Act, for the Procuring & Settling of any such School-Master as aforesaid, by the space of one year. Every such Defective Town shall incur the penalty of Ten Pounds for every Conviction of such Neglect, upon Complaint made unto Their Majesties Justices in Quarter Sessions for the same County, in which such Defective Town lieth; which penalty shall be toward the Support of such School or Schools within the same County, where there may be most need, at the discretion of the Justices in Quarter Sessions; to be Levied by Warrant from the said Court of Sessions in proportion upon the Inhabitants of such Defective Town, as other Publick Charges, and to be paid unto the County Treasurer. *Penalty for Neglect.*

K                     An

## Settling of Bounds

# An Act,

For the Settlement of the Bounds, and Defraying of the Publick and Necessary Charges arising within each Respective County in this Province.

**B**E it Ordained and Enacted by the Governour, Council and Representatives, in General Court Assembled, and by the authority of the same

*Counties to continue as formerly*

That all Counties as they now lye, and are named, continue and remain distinct Counties to all intents and purposes in the Law whatsoever. And that there be a County Treasurer annually Chosen for each Respective County, being a Freeholder within the same; and to be Chosen by the Votes of the Freeholders, and other Inhabitants of each Respective Town, duly qualified as is Provided by the Act for the Choice of Select-men, and other Town Officers; and at the same time, such Votes to be given in Writing, and Sealed up by the Constable, by him to be kept and returned unto the next Quarter Sessions, to be held for said County, there to be Opened and Sorted by such as the Court shall Appoint, in presence of the Justices; and the Person having the Majority of said Votes, shall be Treasurer of such County for that year, and be Sworn before said Court.

*Choice of County-Treasurer*

And for the due and equal Raising of Monies for Defraying of the Charges arising within each Respective County for the necessary Repairs and Amendment of Bridges, Prisons, the Maintainance of poor Prisoners, and all other proper County Charges:

**It is further Enacted by the Authority aforesaid.**

*County Charges, how to be defrayed.*

That when and so often from time to time as there shall be need of raising Mony for the ends aforesaid, in any County; the Justices in Quarter Sessions for such County, receiving Information thereof from the County Treasurer, shall agree and determine the whole Sum to be Raised, and each Respective Towns proportion of the same, as near as may be according to the Rule for Raising of Money for the Province Charges, and shall Issue forth their Order unto the Select-men of the Respective Towns to Assess the same upon the Inhabitants of such Town, each one his due and equal proportion thereof according to the Rule before mentioned, as near as may be, to be paid in Money, or Equivalent thereto; and to make a

distinct

distinct List of each persons name and proportion, under their Hands; and such List Commit unto the Constable or Constables of such Town, with a Warrant Signed by the Town Clerk, directed unto the said Constable or Constables to *Levy* and Collect the said Assessment of each one his respective proportion: And to pay in their said Collections unto the County Treasurer, or his Order, within the time set for the same: And to make distress upon every person neglecting or refusing to make payment: And in default of Goods or Chattels whereon to make Distress, to Commit the Party to the Common Goal of the County, until he make payment, or otherwise be Released by the Justices in Quarter Sessions. And if any person or persons think themselves Over-Rated in any such Assessment, they shall be Eased by the Assessors, making the same to appear; or in default thereof, by the Court of Quarter Sessions.

### And further it is Enacted

That all Monies so Collected, be Improved and Imployed for the Ends within mentioned, as the Court of Quarter Sessions shall from time to time by their Order in Writing, direct and appoint. And the County Treasurer in each respective County, shall Accompt unto the Court of Quarter Sessions, or whom they shall Appoint, for all his Receipts and Payments.

# An Act

## For Regulating of Townships, Choice of Town-Officers, and Setting forth their Power.

**B**e it Ordained and Enacted by the Governour, Council and Representatives in General Court Assembled, and by the authority of the same.

That the Bounds of all Townships shall be, and continue as heretofore Granted and Settled respectively, and shall be run betwixt Town and Town, and Marks Renewed once in three years, by two of the Select-men of each Town, or any other two persons whom the Select-men shall Appoint; the Select-men of the most ancient Town to give Notice unto the Select-men of the next adjacent Towns, of the time and place of Meeting

*Bounds of Townships to continue as heretofore Granted & Setled. And to be run, and Marks Renewed once in 3 years under a penalty.*

for

for such Perambulation, six days before-hand, on pain of Forfeiting Five Pounds by the Select-men of any Town, that shall Neglect their Duty in any of the particulars aforesaid: Two Thirds thereof unto the use of the Poor of such Town; and the other Third unto the Select-Men of any of the next adjacent Towns, that shall Inform and Sue for the same, in the Inferiour Court of Pleas within the same County, to be Recovered by Action or Information.

### And be it further Enacted by the authority aforesaid

*Proprietors of Lands unfenced or in common Fields to run the Lines once in two years.*

That each Proprietor of Lands lying Unfenced, or in any common Field, shall once in two years, on six days warning before given him, by the next Proprietor or Propri:tors adjoyning, run the Lines, make and keep up the Bounds between them, by sufficient met Stones; on pain that every Party so neglecting or refusing, shall Forfeit the Sum of Ten Shillings: one half to the party moving, & the other half to the use of the Poor of the Town, being Convented & Convicted of such Neglect or Refusal, before any Justice of the Peace within the same County, who is hereby Impowred to Hear and Determine the same.

### And further it is Enacted by the authority aforesaid

*Some more Lands, how to be improved.*

That the Proprietors of the Undivided or Common Lands within each Town and Precinct in this Province, where the same have been heretofore Stated, each ones proportion being known, shall, and hereby are Impowred to Order, Improve or Divide in such way and manner as shall be concluded and agreed upon by the major part of the Interested; the Voices to be Collected and Accounted according to the Interests. And the Proprietors of all Undivided or Common Lands not stated and proportioned as aforesaid; shall, and hereby are Impowred to Manage, Improve, Divide or Dispose of the same as hath been, or shall be concluded and agreed on by the major part of such Proprietors. That no Cottage or Dwelling-place in any Town, shall be admitted to the priviledge of Commonage for Woods, Timber and Herbage, or any other the priviledges which lie in Common in any Town, or Peculiar, other than such as were Erected or Priviledged by the Grant of such Town or Peculiar before the Year One Thousand Six Hundred Sixty One, or that have been since, or shall hereafter be Granted by the Consent of any Town or Peculiar.

AND WHEREAS it has been a continued practice and custome in the several Towns within this Province, annually to Choose Select-men or Townsmen, for the ordering and managing of the prudential Affairs of such Town, and other Town-Officers for the Executing of other matters and things, in the Laws appointed by them to be done and performed.

### Be it further Ordained and Enacted by the authority aforesaid

*Qualification of Voters in Town-Meetings.*

That the Freeholders and other Inhabitants of each Town Ratable at Twenty Pounds Estate, to one single Rate besides the Poll; shall some time in the Month of *March* annually meet and convene together upon Notice given by the Constable or Constables of such Town, or such others

## Townships and Town Officers

thers as the Select-men or Towns-men shall appoint, to give Notice of such Meeting, and the time and place for the same: And by the Major Vote of such Assembly, then and there shall Choose Three, Five, Seven, or Nine Persons, Able and Discreet, of good Conversation, Inhabiting within such Town, to be Select-men or Townsmen, and Overseers of the Poor, where other persons shall not be particularly Chosen to that Office (which any Town may do as they shall find it necessary and convenient) as also to Nominate and Choose a Town-Clerk, who shall be Sworn truly to Enter and Record all Town-Votes, Orders, Grants and Divisions of Land, made by such Town, and Orders made by the Select-men; a Commissioner for Assessments, Constables, Surveyers of High-ways, Tything-men, Fence-viewers, Clerks of the Market, Sealers of Leather, and other ordinary Town Officers: And the Town-Clerk, or two of the Select-men, shall forthwith make, and give out unto the Constable or Constables of such Town, a List of the Names of those that shall be then Chosen to the Office of Town Clerk, Constables, Tything-men, Clerks of the Market, Sealers of Leather, and other Officers, of whom an Oath is by Law required; which Constable or Constables within the space of six days at furthest, shall Summon each of them respectively to appear before the Quarter Sessions, if then Sitting, or one of the next Justices of the Peace, to be Sworn to the faithful Discharge of their Respective Offices and Trust, on penalty of Twenty Shillings to the use of the Poor of the Town, to be paid by each Constable neglecting of his Duty in that behalf, upon Conviction thereof before one Justice of the Peace; and upon Non Payment, to be Levied by Distress. PROVIDED That no Person in Commission for any Office, Civil or Military, Church-Officer, or Member of the House of Representatives for the time being, nor any other who has Served as Constable within the space of seven years before, shall be Chosen to the Office of Constable.

*Select-men, Constables and other Town Officers to be Chosen annually in March.*

*Town Clerk to be under Oath.*

*Constables to Summon Town Officers to be Sworn under a penalty.*

*Persons exempted from Serving as Constables.*

**It is further Enacted by the Authority aforesaid,**

That the Freeholders and Inhabitants qualified as in this Act is mentioned in each Respective Town, in any Town-Meeting, orderly warned according to the Usage in such Town, or the major part so Assembled, or the Select-men having Instructions given them in Writing by the Town for that purpose; Be, and hereby are Impowred from time to time to make and agree upon such necessary Rules, Orders and By-Laws for the directing, managing and ordering the Prudential Affairs of such Town, as they shall judge most Conducing to the Peace, Welfare and good Order thereof, and to annex Penalties for the observance of the same, not exceeding Twenty Shillings for one Offence, Provided that they be not repugnant to the General Laws of the Province: And such Orders and By-Laws being presented unto the Justices in Quarter Sessions, and approved of by them, shall be Established, and Binding to all the Inhabitants of such Town, and the penalty for breach of any of them by any of the Inhabitants, to be Levied by Warrant of Distress from any Justice of the Peace before

*Towns or Select-men having Instructions, to make Orders & By-Laws.*

*Orders and By-Laws in Towns, to be approved by the Quarter Sessions. Penalty to be Levied by Warrant from a Justice*

whom such Offender shall be Convicted, to the use of the Poor of such Town.

***And further it is Enacted by the Authority aforesaid.***

**Select-men to make Assessment for County and Town Charges**

That the Select-men or Townsmen Chosen as aforesaid, in each Town respectively, Be, and hereby are Impowred to assess the Inhabitants and others Resident within such Town, and the Precincts thereof, and the Lands and Estates lying within the Bounds of such Town, in just and equal proportion as near as may be unto the County Charges, according as they shall receive order from the Court of Quarter Sessions, to be held for the same County; and to all Town Charges, each particular person according to his known Ability and Estate, such Sum and Sums as hath or shall be ordered, granted and agreed upon from time to time by the Inhabitants in any Town-Meeting regularly Assembled; or the major part of those present at such Meeting, for the Maintainance and Support of the Ministry, Schools, the Poor, and for the defraying of other necessary Charges arising within the said Town; and thereof to make distinct and perfect Lists under their Hands, or the major part of them, setting down every persons Name, and several proportion, and shall thereupon make out a Warrant to be Signed by the said Assessors, or the Town Clerk, by their Order (who are hereby respectively Impowred thereto) directed unto the Constable or Constables of the said Town for the speedy Levying and Collecting of such Assesments, and to pay in the same unto the Select-men, or to such person as they shall appoint for Receiver, within the time thereby prefixt. And to make Distress upon all such who shall neglect or refuse to make payment: And for want of Goods or Chattels whereon to make Distress, to Seiz the person and Commit him to the Common Goal of the County, there to remain until he pay the Sum upon him Assessed as aforesaid; unless the same or any part thereof, upon application made unto the Quarter Sessions, shall be Abated. And if any person think himself Over-rated, and make it so appear unto the Assessors, he shall be Eased: And if they refuse, such person agrieved may make his Application unto the Justices in Quarter Sessions, who are hereby Impowred to Rectifie the same: And all Constables having any such Assessment committed unto them, shall Settle and Issue their Accompts thereof with the Select-men, or Receiver appointed by them, within three months after their time or year is Expired, on pain of Forfeiting the Sum of Twenty Shillings *per* Month, for each Months Neglect afterward, to the use of the Poor of such Town, and to be Levied by Distress upon such Delinquent Constables Goods, by Warrant from one Justice of the Peace, being Convented and Convicted of such Neglect before him, who is hereby thereto Impowred.

Provided nevertheless, that every Constable at the end of every Three Months shall pay in as aforesaid, so much as he shall have Collected within that time.

*And*

## Townships & Town Officers 41

### And it is further Enacted by the Authority aforesaid,

That the Select-men or Overseers of the Poor in each Town ( where there are such Chosen, and specially Appointed for that Service ) are hereby Impowred and Ordered to take effectual care that all Children, Youth, and other persons of able Body, living within the same Town or Precincts thereof ( not having Estates otherwise to Maintain themselves ) do not live Idly, or misspend their time in Loitering, but that they be brought up or imployed in some honest Calling, which may be profitable unto themselves, and the Publick. And if any person or persons fit and able to work, shall refuse so to do, but loiter & misspend his or her time, wander from place to place, or otherwise misorder themselves; and thereof be Convicted before one or more Justices of the Peace, such person or persons shall by such Justice or Justices be sent to the House of Correction, and at their Entrance, be whipped on the naked back, by the Master of such House, or such other as he shall procure, not exceeding Ten Lashes; and be there kept to hard Labour, until he or she be discharged by such Justice or Justices, or the Quarter Sessions of the Peace for the same County: And it shall, and may be lawful for the Overseers of the Poor, or Select-men in each Town, where there are no other persons specially Chosen and Appointed to be Overseers of the Poor, and they are hereby Ordered with the Assent of two Justices of the Peace, to Bind any poor Children belonging to such Town, to be Apprentices, where they shall see convenient; a Man Child, until he shall come to the Age of Twenty One Years, and a Woman Child, to the Age of Eighteen Years, or time of Marriage: which shall be as effectual to all Intents and purposes, as if any such Child were of full Age, and by Indenture of Covenant had Bound him or her self.

*Idle Persons and Loiterers to be Imployed. Upon refusal to labour, to be sent to the House of Correction.*

*Poor Children to be bound out Apprentices.*

### And it is further Enacted by the Authority aforesaid,

That every person and persons, ( except as in this Act is before excepted ) being duly Chosen as aforesaid, to Serve in the Office of Constable, who shall refuse to take the Oath to that Office belonging, and to Serve therein, if he be able in Person to Execute the same, shall pay the Sum of Five Pounds, to the use of the Poor of such Town. And if in the Towns of *Boston* or *Salem*, the Sum of Ten Pounds, and shall forthwith declare his acceptance or refusal, and the Town shall proceed to a new Choice, and if such person refuse to pay down his Fine, he shall be Convented before the next Sessions of the Peace, to be held for that County, in which such Town lieth, who upon Certificate under the Hand of the Town Clerk, or two or more of the Select-men, that such person was Legally Chosen to the Office of Constable, and shewing no just cause to the Sessions for his Excuse; the Justices shall Order a Warrant to be Signed by the Clerk of the Peace, directed to any of the Constables then in being

*Penalty for not Serving in the Office of Constable*

within

within such Town, to Levy the said Fine by Distress and Sale of such Offenders Goods, returning the Over-plus (if any be) said Fine to be Delivered unto the Overseers of the Poor, or Select men, to the Use of the Poor of such Town.

### And be it further Enacted by the Authority aforesaid,

*Persons Entertained in any Town by the space of 3 months, and not warned out, to be reputed Inhabitants.*

*Persons of Ability, to relieve their poor Relations.*

That if any person or persons come to Sojourn or Dwell in any Town within this Province, or Precincts thereof, and be there Received and Entertained by the space of Three Months, not having been warned by the Constable, or other Person whom the Select-men shall Appoint for that Service, to leave the place, and the names of such persons, with the time of their Abode there, and when such warning was given them, returned unto the Court of Quarter Sessions; every such person shall be Reputed an Inhabitant of such Town or Precincts of the same; and the proper Charge of the same, in case through Sickness, Lameness, or otherwise they come to stand in need of Relief, to be born by such Town; Unless the Relations of such poor impotent person, in the Line or Degree of Father, or Grand-father, Mother or Grand-Mother, Children or Grand-Children, be of sufficient ability; then such Relations respectively shall Relieve such poor person, in such manner as the Justices of the Peace in that County where such sufficient Persons Dwell, shall Assess; on pain that every one failing therein, shall Forfeit Twenty Shillings for every Months Neglect, to be Levied by Distress and Sale of such Offenders Goods by Warrant from any two such Justices of the Peace (*Quorum Unus*) within their Limits; which shall be imployed to the Use and Relief of such impotent poor person. PROVIDED nevertheless this Act shall not be understood of any persons Committed to Prison, or lawfully Restrained in any Town, or of such as shall come, or be sent for Nursing or Education; or to any Physician or Chirurgeon to be Healed or Cured; but the particular persons who Receive and Entertain any such, shall be the Towns Security in their behalf; and be obliged to Relieve and Support them in case of need; upon Complaint made to the Quarter Sessions, who shall accordingly Order the same.

### And it is further Enacted by the Authority aforesaid,

*Persons warned out of any Town; to depart in 14 days or else to be sent by the Constable.*

That any person orderly warned as aforesaid to depart any Town whereof he is not an Inhabitant, and Neglecting so to do by the space of Fourteen Days next after such warning given, may by Warrant from the next Justice of the Peace be sent and conveyed from Constable to Constable, unto the Town where he properly belongs, or had his last Residence, at his own Charge, if able to pay the same, or otherwise at the Charge of the Town so sending him.

and

# Lands and Tenements liable to Pay Debts 43

**And further it is Enacted by the Authority aforesaid,**

That when and so often as there shall be occasion of a Town-Meeting for any Business of Publick Concernment to the Town, there to be done. The Constable or Constables of such Town, by order from the Select-men, or major part of them, or of the Town Clerk by their Order, in each Respective Town within this Province shall warn a Meeting of such Town, having order for the same in Writing; on pain that every Constable neglecting his Duty in that respect; and being thereof Convicted before one Justice of the Peace, shall Forfeit the Sum of Twenty Shillings, to the Use of the Poor of such Town, and to be Levied by Distress and Sale of such Offenders Goods, by Warrant from such Justice of the Peace, upon Neglect or Refusal of payment. And in case the Select-men in any Town shall unreasonably deny to call a Meeting of the Inhabitants of such Town, upon any Publick Occasion thereof, the same being Complained of and made to appear to one of the next Justices of the Peace within the same County; such Justice by his Warrant directed to the Constable or Constables, may order a Meeting of the Inhabitants of such Town, therein signifying the occasion thereof.

*Constables to warn Town-Meetings.*

*Penalty for Neglect.*

*Justice to give Warrant for Town-Meeting in case.*

## An Act,

### For making of Lands and Tenements liable to the Payment of Debts.

WHEREAS the Estates of Persons within this Provnince do chiefly consist of Houses and Lands, which give them Credit, some being remiss in paying of their just Debts; others happening to Dye before they have discharged the same.

**It is therefore Ordained and Enacted by the Governour, Council and Representatives, Convened in General Court, and by the Authority of the same,**

That all Lands or Tenements belonging to any person in his own proper right in Fee Simple, shall stand charged with the payment of all just Debts owing by such person, as well as his personal Estate, and shall be liable to be taken in Execution for satisfaction of the same, where
the

the Debtor, or his Attourney shall not Expose to view, and Tender to the Officer Personal Estate sufficient to answer the Sum mentioned in the Execution with the Charges. And all Executions duly Served upon any such Houses and Lands, being Returned into the Clerk's Office of the Court, out of which the same Issued, and there Recorded, shall make a good Title to the Party, for whom they are so taken, his Heirs and Assigns for ever.

<small>Superiour Court may Impower Executors, Administrators to Sell Land for payment of Debts.</small>

Also where the Goods and Moveables of any person Deceased shall not be sufficient to answer the just Debts which the Deceased owed: Upon Representation thereof, and making the same to appear unto the Superiour Court within the County where such Deceased Person last Dwelt; the said Court are hereby Impowred to Licence and Authorize the Executor or Administrator of such Person Deceased to make Sale of all or any part of the Houses and Lands of the Deceased, so far as shall be necessary to satisfie the just Debts which the Deceased Owed at the time of his Death. And every Executor, or Administrator being so Licenced and Authorized, shall, and may by virtue of such Authority Make and Execute Deeds or Conveyances in due Form for such Houses and Lands as they shall so Sell, which Instruments shall be a good Title to the Purchaser.

### And further it is Enacted by the Authority aforesaid.

That where any person shall make Sale or other Alienation of any Lands or Tenements to him of right belonging, with Intent to Defeat and Defraud his Creditors of their just Debts, not *Bona Fide* for good and valuable consideration paid. All such Sales and Alienations are to be deemed Covenous and Fraudulent, and shall be of none Effect to Bar any Creditor from such Debt as is to him Owing.

# An Act

### For due Regulation of Weights and Measures.

TO the end that Weights and Measures may be one and the same throughout this Their Majesties Province.

**Be it Enacted and Ordained by the Governour, Council and Representatives, in General Court Assembled, and by the Authority of the same,**

That the Brass and Copper Weights and Measures formerly sent out of *England*, with Certificate out of Their Majesties Exchequer, to be approved *Winchester* Measure according to the Standard in the Exchequer, be the publick allowed Standard throughout this Their Majesties Province, for the Proving and Sealing all Weights and Measures thereby; And the Constables of every Town throughout this Province, not already Supplied, shall within three Months next coming, provide upon the Towns Charge; One Bushel, one half Bushel, one Peck, one Half Peck, one Ale Quart, one Wine-pint and Half-pint, One Ell, one Yard, one Sett of Brass Weights, to Four Pounds, after sixteen Ounces to the Pound, with fit Scales, and Steel Beam, tried and proved by the aforesaid Standard, and Sealed by the Treasurer, or his Deputy in his Presence, ( which shall be kept and used only for Standards in the several Towns ) who is hereby Authorized to do the same, for which he shall receive from the Constables of each Town Two-pence for every Weight and Measure so Tried and Proved and Sealed. And the Constables of every Town shall Commit those Weights and Measures unto the Custody of the Select-men of their Towns for the time being, who with the Constables are hereby Enjoyned to Choose one Able Man for Sealer of all Weights and Measures for their Town from time to time, and till another be Chose, who shall be presented unto the next Court of Sessions, and there Sworn to the faithful Discharge of his Duty; And shall have power to send forth his Warrants by the Constable to all the Inhabitants of such Town, to bring in all such Weights and Measures as they make use of, in the Month of *April*, from year to year, at such time and place as he shall appoint, and make Return to the Sealer in Writing of all persons so Summoned. That then and there all such Weights and Measures may be Proved and Sealed with the Town Seal ( which is likewise to be provided by the Constables at each Towns Charge ) who shall have for every Weight and Measure so Sealed, one penny from the Owner thereof at the first Sealing. And all such Weights

Weights and Measures as cannot be brought to their juſt Standard, he ſhall Deface and Deſtroy, and after the firſt Sealing, ſhall have nothing, ſo long as they continue juſt with the Standard.

### And it is further Enacted by the authority aforeſaid.

That if any Conſtable, Selectman or Sealer, do not duly Execcute this Law ſo far as to each & every of them appertains, they & each of them ſhall Forfeit to Their Majeſties for every ſuch Neglect, by the ſpace of one Month the Sum of Forty Shillings, towards the Support of their Government here. And every perſon Neglecting to bring in their Weights & Meaſures at the time and place appointed, being duly warned thereto, ſhall likewiſe Forfeit Three Shillings and Four-pence; the one half whereof to be to Their Majeſties as aforeſaid, the other half to the Sealer aforeſaid. And the penalty herein mentioned, to be Levied by Diſtreſs by Warrant from any Juſtice of the Peace.

### And it is further Enacted by the authority aforeſaid.

That in every Sea-port-Town within this Province, the Conſtable or Conſtables are to provide upon the Towns Charge, One Hundred Weight, one Half Hundred, one Quarter of an Hundred, and one Fourteen Pounds Weight made of Iron, to be Tried, Proved and Sealed as aforeſaid, and be kept as Standards in the ſaid ſeveral Towns to be uſed as before for other Weights and Meaſures is directed.

An

# An Act,

Against the Counterfeiting, Clipping, Rounding, Filing or Impairing of Coynes.

**W**HEREAS divers False and Evil Disposed Persons have attempted and practised for Wicked Lucre and Gains sake, to Diminish Impair and Falsifie the Money, and Coynes Currant within this Province, by Counterfeiting or Clipping, Rounding, or Filing thereof, not only to the great Discredit of the Province, and the Government thereof, but also to the great Loss and Damage of Their Majesties Subjects; and more is like to be if the same be not speedily met withal and prevented.

For Remedy whereof,

**B**e it Enacted, and Declared, and Established, by the Governour, Council and Representatives, in General Court Assembled, and by the Authority of the same.

That the Coyn of the Late Massachusetts Colony, shall pass currant at the rate it was Stampt for. *Massachusetts Coyn, & pieces of Eight,*

And Pieces of Eight, Sevil, Pillar, and Mexico, of full Seventeen penny Weight, shall pass Currant at Six Shillings *Per* Piece, and Half Pieces of Due Weight *Pro Rato*, and Quarter Pieces of the same Coin, at Sixteen pence *Per* Piece, and Realls, of the same Coin, at Eight Pence *Per* piece. *of 17 penny weight made currant.*

And whosoever from and after the Publication of this Act, shall Attempt and Practice the Counterfeiting, or Clipping, Rounding, Filing, or otherwise Diminishing, or Debasing any of the Monies and Coins Currant within this Province; being thereof Lawfully Convicted before the Justices of Assize; shall Forfeit double the value of the Money, so Counterfeited, Clipped, Rounded or Filed; One Half to Their Majesties towards the Support of the Government; And the other Half to the Informer. And shall also stand in the Pillory, in some open Place in the Shire Town, of that County where the Offence is Committed; and there have one of His Ears Cut off. *Penalty for Counterfeiting, Clipping &c. of Coyns.*

An Act,

# An Act,

For the Regulating and Encouragement of Fishery.

Upon Consideration of great Damage and Scandal, That hath happened upon the account of Pickled Fish, although afterwards Dried and hardly discoverable; To the great Loss of many, and also an ill Reputation on this Province, and the Fishery of it.

**Be it therefore Enacted, by the Governour, Council, and Representatives, Convened in General Court, or Assembly, and it is Enacted by the Authority** of the same.

*No Mackerel to be Salted up before the first of July.*

*How dry Fish shall be Saved.*

That no person or persons whatsoever, after the Publication hereof, shall Save or Salt any sort of Fish (that is intended to be dried) in Cask or Fattes, or any other way) then what hath formerly and honestly been practised for the making of dry Fish, on penalty of Forfeiting all such Fish, so Salted and Pickled, whether it be Green or Drye: The one Moiety thereof to the use of the Poor of the Town, where the Offence is Committed, and the other Moiety to the person that shall Sue for the same.

**And it is further Enacted by the authority aforesaid.**

*Penalty for Taking Mackarel in Netts or Seynes*

That henceforth no Mackrel shall be Caught (except for spending whilst fresh) before the first of *July* annually: And no person or persons whatsoever after the publication hereof, shall at any time or place within this Province, Take, Kill, or Hale ashore any Mackrell, with any sort of Nets or Sa'ens whatsoever, on penalty of Forfeiting all such Mackrel so Taken or Haled ashore, and also all such Nets and Sa'ens which were so Imployed: The one half thereof to Their Majesties, towards the Support of this their Government, and the other half to him or them that shall Inform and Sue for the same. And all Justices are hereby Impowred, and Required, to Grant their Warrants for the Seizing of the same, and the aforesaid Forfeitures, or the Receiving of the like value in Currant Mony of this Province,

*An*

# An Act,

## For the Establishing of Judicatories, & Courts of Justice, within this Province.

For the more Orderly Regulation and Establishment of Courts of Justice, throughout this Province.

**Be it Enacted, and Ordained by His Excellency the Governour, Council, and Representatives, Convened in General Assembly.**

**And it is hereby Enacted, and Ordained, by the Authority of the same.**

That all manner of Debts, Trespasses, and other Matters not exceeding the value of Forty Shillings, ( wherein the Title of Land is not Concerned ) shall and may be heard, Tryed, Adjudged, and Determined, by any of Their Majesties Justices of the Peace, of this Province, within the Respective Countys where he resides; Who is hereby Impowred, upon complaint made, to grant a Warrant or Summons, against the Party complained of, Seven Days before the day of Tryall or Hearing, thereby requiring him or them to appear and answer the said Complaint, and in case of *Non-Appearance*, to Issue out a Warrant of Contempt, directed to the Constable or other Officer, to bring the Contemner before him, as well to answer the said Contempt, as the Plaintiffs Action, and if he see cause to Fine the said Contemner. 

*Justices Court*

PROVIDED the said Fine Exceed not Ten Shillings, to be accounted for to the Treasurer of the County, towards the Support of the Government, and after Judgment given in either Case, may grant Warrants of Distress, directed to the Constable or other Officer to Levy the said Fine, debt or damage with Charges, upon the Defendants Goods and Chattels, who by vertue thereof shall expose the same to Sale, returning the Overplus ( if any be ) to the Defendant. And for want of such Distress to take the Body of such Defendant into Custody, and him to carry and convey to the common Goal, of the County or Precinct, there to remain, until he hath satisfyed the Said Fine, Debt or Damage, with Charges.

And in case such Complainant be Non-Suited, or Judgment pass against him, then the said Justice is hereby Impowred to Assess to the Defendant, reasonable Costs against such Complainant, to be Levied and recovered in manner & form above Expressed.

And the said Justice is hereby required to keep fair Records of all his proceedceedings therein from time to time. Provided always nevertheleſs, That the Party Caſt ſhall have Liberty to Appeal to the next Inferiour Court of Common Pleas, to be Holden for the ſame County, He entring into Recognizance with one ſufficient Suretie in double the value of the Debt or Damage Sued for, and ſufficient to anſwer all Coſts to proſecute the ſaid Appeal there with Effect, and to abide the Order of the ſaid Court; where ſuch Caſe ſhall be Tryed, there to receive a Final Iſſue. Provided alſo, That the party Appealing, ſhall bring the Copies of the whole Caſe to ſaid Court; and each party ſhall be there allowed the benefit of any further Plea or Evidence. And if upon any ſuch new Plea or Evidence, the Judgement happen to be Reverſed, the Appellant ſhall have no Coſts Granted for the firſt Tryal.

### Be it further Enacted and Ordained by the authority aforeſaid

*Quarter Seſſions of the Peace*

That there ſhall be Held and Kept in each Reſpective County within this Province yearly, at the times and places hereafter named and expreſſed: Four Courts or Quarter Seſſions of the Peace, by the Juſtices of the Peace of the ſame County, who are hereby Impowred to Hear and Determine all Matters relating to the Conſervation of the Peace, and Puniſhment of Offenders, and whatſoever is by them Cognizeable according to Law. That is to ſay, For the County of *Suffolk*, at *Boſton* on the firſt *Tueſdays* in *March, June, September* and *December*. For the County of *Plymouth*, at *Plymouth*, on the third *Tueſdayes* in *March, June, September* and *December*: For the County of *Eſſex*, at *Salem*, on the laſt *Tueſdayes* in *June* and *December*; at *Ipſwich*, on the laſt *Tueſday* in *March*, and at *Newbury*, on the laſt *Tueſday* in *September*: For the County of *Middleſex*, at *Charleſtown*, on the ſecond *Tueſdayes* in *March* and *December*; at *Cambridge*, on the ſecond *Tueſday* in *September*, and at *Concord* on the ſecond *Tueſday* of *June*: For the County of *Barnſtable*, at *Barnſtable*, on the firſt *Tueſdayes* in *April, July, October* and *January*. At *Briſtol*, for the County of *Briſtol*, on the ſecond *Tueſdays* in *April, July, October* and *January*. For the County of *York*, at *York*, on the Firſt *Tueſdayes* in *April* and *July*; and at *Wells*, on the firſt *Tueſdayes* in *October* and *January*; and for the County of *Hampſhire*, at *North-hampton*, on the Firſt *Tueſdayes* in *March* and *June*; at *Springfield* on the laſt *Tueſdayes* in *September* and *December*; and that there be a General Seſſions of the Peace Held and Kept at *Edgar* Town upon the Iſland of *Capawock, alias Martha's* Vineyard, and on the Iſland of *Nantucket* reſpectively, upon the laſt *Tueſday* in *March*, and on the firſt *Tueſday* of *October* yearly from time to time.

### And it is further Enacted by the Authority aforeſaid

*Courts of Common Pleas*

That at the times and places before mentioned, there ſhall be Held and

## Judicatories & Courts of Justice 51

and kept in each Respective County and Islands before-named within this Province, an Interiour Court of Common Pleas, by four of the Justices of, and Residing within the same County, and Islands respectively, to be appointed and commissionated thereto; any Three of whom to be a *Quorum*, for the hearing and determining of all Civil Actions, arising or hapning within the same, tryable at the common Law; of what nature, kind, or quality soever; and upon judgment given therein, to award Execution.

*Appeal to the Superiour Court*

PROVIDED nevertheless That it shall be in the Liberty of the party cast in any of the said Inferiour Courts, to Appeal from the Verdict and Judgment given therein, unto the next Superiour Court, to be held within, or for the same County; the case there to be Tryed to a Final Issue. Or by a new Process, once and no more, to review the said case in the same Court, where it was first Tryed; and within the space of ten days, after judgment given upon such Tryall, by review; the party agrieved may bring his Writt of Error, for a Tryall of the said Case at the next Superiour Court, to be held within or for the same County, there to receive a Final Issue and Determination.

*Review*

PROVIDED also, that the Party Appealing, or bringing any Writt of Error as aforesaid; shall first enter into Recognizance, with sufficient Sureties, before one or more of the Justices of the Court appealed from, and upon Writt of Error, before one or more of the Justices of the Superiour Court in double the value of the Debt or Damage recovered that he will prosecute the same Appeal or Writt respectively with effect, and abide the Order of the Court; no Appeal to be admitted after the time of the Courts Sitting, nor after Execution Granted; and the Party Appealing, to bring the Copies of the whole Case unto the Superiour Court, where each Party shall be allowed the benefit of any new and further Plea & Evidence. And if upon any such new Plea and Evidence, the Judgement happen to be Reversed, the Appellant shall have no Cost granted him for the first Tryal.

PROVIDED also, That every Appellant as aforesaid, shall give in a Declaration, briefly setting forth the Reasons of his Appeal, unto the Clerk of the Court Appealed from, fourteen days inclusively before the Sitting of that Court, where such Appeal is to be Tryed.

### And it is further Enacted by the authority aforesaid,

*Superiour Court*

That there shall be a Superiour Court of Judicature over this whole Province, to be Held and Kept annually at the Respective Times and Places hereafter mentioned, by one Chief Justice, and four other Justices, to be Appointed and Commissionated for the same; Three of whom to be a *Quorum*, who shall have Cognizance of all Pleas, Real, Personal, or Mixt, as well in all Pleas of the Crown, and in all Matters Relating to the Conservation of the Peace, and Punishment of Offenders, as in Civil Causes or Actions between Party and Party, and between Their Majesties,

and

and any of their Subjects; whether the same do Concern the Realty, and Relate to any Right of Freehold and Inheritance, or whether the same do concern the Personalty, and Relate to matter of Debt, Contract, Damage, or Personal Injury; and also in all Mixt Actions, which may Concern both Realty and Personalty; and after Deliberate Hearing, to give Judgment, and Award Execution thereon. The said Superiour Court to be Held and Kept at the times and places within the Respective Counties following: *That is to say*, within the County of *Suffolk*, At *Boston*, on the last *Tuesdayes* of *April* and *October*. Within the County of *Middlesex*, at *Charlstown*, on the last *Tuesdayes* of *July* and *January*: Within the County of *Essex*, at *Salem*, on the Second *Tuesday* of *November*; and at *Ipswich*, on the Second *Tuesday* of *May*. Within the Counties of *Plimouth*, *Barnstable* and *Bristol*: At *Plimouth*, on the last *Tuesday* of *February*, and at *Bristol*, on the last *Tuesday* of *August*.

## And be it further Enacted by the authority aforesaid.

That the Tryal of all Civil Causes by Appeal, or Writ of Error, from any of the Inferiour Courts within the Respective Counties of *York* or *Hampshire*, the Islands of *Capawock*, alias, *Martha's*-Vineyard, and *Nantucket*, shall be in the Superiour Court to be Held at *Boston*, or *Charlstown*.

## And further it is Enacted

Court of Assize & General Goal Delivery

That when, and in what County soever, the said Superiour Court shall Sit, the Justices thereof shall Hold a Court of Assize, and General Goal Delivery for the said County, at the same time, as occasion shall be. And there shall be Held and Kept a Court of Assize, and General Goal Delivery, for the Respective Counties and Places of *York*, *Hampshire*, the Islands of *Capawock*. alias, *Martha's*-Vineyard and *Nantucket* within the same from time to time, as the Governour and Council, advising with the Justices of the Superiour Court, shall Direct and Appoint, according as occasion may be.

## And it is further Enacted by the authority aforesaid.

Plaintiffs liberty to begin his Suit in the Inferiour or Superiour Court.

That it shall be in the Liberty of any Plaintiff, to begin his Suit, either in the Inferiour or Superiour Court, at his pleasure; and where the Original Process is made out of the Superiour Court, the Party Cast shall have Liberty to Review his Case in the said Superiour Court, once and no more. PROVIDED Nevertheless, That none of the said Inferiour Courts shall Receive any Action under the value of Forty Shillings;

## Judicatories & Courts of Justice    53

lings; nor shall any Action under the value of Ten Pounds be brought into the Superiour Court, unless where Freehold is concerned, or upon Appeal.

*No Action under Ten Pounds to come originally to the Superiour Court.*

### And it is further Enacted by the Authority aforesaid,

That all Matters and Issues in Fact arising, or happening within the said Province, shall be Tryed by Twelve Good and Lawful Men of the Neighbourhood. And that no person or persons shall be Chosen and Returned to Serve upon any such Jury, but such as shall have a Real Estate of Freehold worth Forty Shillings *per Annum*, or Personal Estate worth Fifty Pounds. And for the more equal returning and appearance of Jurors to serve in the several Courts.

*Matters of Fact to be Tryed by a Jury.*

### It is Enacted by the Authority aforesaid

That the Clerk of each Court respectively, in convenient time, before the Sitting of such Court, shall Issue out Warrants directed to the Constables of the several Towns within the County, or Jurisdiction of said Court, or the most principal of them, to Assemble the Freeholders and other Inhabitants of each several Town, qualified as aforesaid, to Serve as Jurors; Requiring them to Choose so many good and lawful Men as the Warrant shall direct for Grand and Petit Jurors to serve at such Court, and the Constable shall Summon the Persons so Chosen, to attend accordingly, at the time and place appointed; and make timely Return of his Warrant unto the Clerk that Granted the same. And no Person Serving as a Justice, Juror, Witness, or otherwise, shall be obliged to use any other Ceremony in taking of their Respective Oaths, then lifting up the Hand as has been accustomed.

*Jurors how to be Chosen*

### And be it further Enacted by the Authority aforesaid.

That all Processes and Writs shall Issue out of the Clerks Office of the said Respective Courts in Their Majesties Names, under the Seal of the said Office; and Signed by the Clerk, and be directed to the Sheriff or Marshal of the County, his Under-Sheriff or Deputy. And where the Sum Sued for is under Ten Pounds, to direct also to the Constable of the Town.

*All Processes and Writs to Issue forth in Their Majesties Names Town-Clerk to grant Attachments for*

PROVIDED Nevertheless, That Replevins Summons and Attachments for any matter or cause Tryable before one Justice of the Peace; and Summons for Witnesses in civil Cases, may be Granted by the Town Clerk

*Cases tryable before one Justice, and Summons for Witnesses*

Clerk, and directed to the Constable of such Town, or to the Party to be Summoned for Witness. And the Clerk of each Town respectively within this Province, is hereby Impowred, to Make and Grant such Writs and Processes as aforesaid; and the Constable or Constables of such Town are Required to Execute them. And all Processes for Appearance, as well in the Inferiour Court of Pleas, as the Superiour Court of Judicature, shall be Served and Executed fourteen days before the Sitting of such Court, wherein such Writs shall be returnable; and that all proper Original Processes in the said Courts, shall be Summons, Capias or Attachment. And in case upon any such Summons duly Served, and Affidavit thereof made in Court, the Defendant do not appear by himself or his Attourney lawfully Authorized, Judgment shall pass against him by Default.

### And it is further Enacted and Declared by the Authority aforesaid

*Justices of Courts to make necessary Rules & Orders.*

That the Justices of the said several Courts be, and hereby are Impowred to make necessary Rules and Orders for the more orderly practising and proceeding in said Courts; and that no Summons, Process, Writ, Judgment, or other Proceeding in Courts, or course of Justice, shall be abated, arrested or reversed upon any kind of Circumstantial Errors or Mistakes where the person and case may be rightly understood and intended by the Court, nor through defect or want of form only. And all Writs, Processes, Declarations, Pleas, Answers, Replications and Entries in all the said Courts shall be in the *English* Tongue and no other. And that it shall be in the Liberty of every Plaintiff or Defendant in any of the said Courts, to Plead and Defend his own Cause in his proper person, or with the Assistance of such other as he shall procure, being a person not Scandalous or otherwise offensive to the Court.

### And it is hereby further Enacted by the authority aforesaid

*Court of Chancery.*

That there be a High Court of Chancery within this Province, who shall have Power and Authority to Hear and Determine all Matters of Equity of what nature, kind or quality soever, and all Controversies, Disputes and Differences arising betwixt Co-Executors, and other Matters proper and Cognizeable to said Court, not Relievable by common Law; the said Court to be Holden and Kept by the Governour, or such other as He shall Appoint to be Chancellor, Assisted with Eight or more of the Council, who may appoint all necessary Officers to the said Court; which said Court shall Sit and be Held at such times and places as the Governour or Chancellor for the time being, shall from time to time Appoint.

PROVIDED Nevertheless, That the Justices in any of the Courts aforesaid,

## Judicatories & Courts of Justice

aforesaid, where the Forfeiture of any Penal Bond is found, shall be and hereby are Impowred to Chancer the same unto the just Debt and Damages.

Provided also, That either Party not resting satisfied with the Judgment or Sentence of any of the said Judicatories or Courts in pecuniall Cases where in the matter in Difference doth exceed the value of Three Hundred Pounds Sterling ( and no other ) may Appeal unto Their Majesties in Councill, the Appeal being made in time, and Security given according to the Directions in the Charter in that behalf. Appeal to Their Majesties in Councill.

### And it is further Enacted by the authority aforesaid,

That Two Shillings *Per Diem* shall be accounted due satisfaction to any Witness for his Travel and Expences, and no more, to be allowed in civil Causes; and if such Witness live within Three Miles of the Place of the Courts Sitting whereto he is Summoned, and be not to pass any Ferry, then One Shilling and Six pence *Per Diem* shall be accounted sufficient: And if any person or persons upon whom any Process out of any Court of Record shall be Served, to Testifie or Depose concerning any Cause or matter Depending in any of the same Courts, and having tendred unto him or them such reasonable Sums of Mony for his or their Costs and Charges, as having regard to the distance of the places, is necessary to be allowed in that behalf, do not appear according to the Tenor of the Process, having no lawful or reasonable Let or Impediment to the contrary; that then the party so making Default, shall for every such Offence Lose and Forfeit Forty Shillings, and shall yield such further Recompence to the Party grieved, as by the Discretion of the Justices of the Court out of which such Process Issued, shall be Awarded, according to the Loss and Hindrance that the Party which procured the said Process shall sustain, by reason of the Non Appearance of the said Witness or Witnesses; the said several Sums to be Recovered by the Party so grieved, against the Offender or Offenders, by Action of Debt, Bill, Plaint or Information in any of Their Majesties Courts of Record, in which no Wager of Law, Essoign or Protection to be Allowed. Witnesses allowance.<br/><br/>Penalty for Non-appearance.

### It is further Declared and Enacted by the authority aforesaid.

That every Justice of the Peace may Grant Summons, Capias or Attachment in all Civil Actions Triable before him. Justices may Grant Summons, Capias or Attachment.

# An Act,

Requiring the Taking the Oaths, appointed to be taken inftead of the Oaths of Allegiance, and Supremacy.

**WHEREAS** Their Royal Majefties in and by Their Charter for the Erecting and Incorporating of Their Province, of the *Maffachufetts-Bay*, in *New-England* **Have Granted and Ordained,** That the Governour, or Lieutenant, or Deputy Governour, of Their faid Province, or Territory, for the time being, or either of them or any Two or more of the Council or Affiftants for the time being, as fhall be thereunto appointed by the faid Governour, fhall and may at all times, and from time to time, have full Power, & Authority, to Adminifter, & Give the Oaths, appointed by an Act of Parliament made in the Firft Year of Their prefent Majefties Reign (Entituled An Act for the Abrogating of the Oaths of Allegiance and Supremacy, and appointing other Oaths) to be taken ftead of the Oaths of Allegiance and Supremacy; to all and every perfon and Perfons, which are now Inhabiting, or Refiding within the faid Province or Territory; Or which fhall at any time or times, hereafter go or pafs thither.

Now to the Intent that there be no failure herein, but that Their Majefties Subjects within this Their Province, may accordingly Recognize their Duty, and Allegiance.

**Be it Enacted and Ordained by His Excellency the Governour, Council, and Reprefentatives, in General Court Affembled.**
**And by the Authority of the fame.**

*All male perfons of 18 years and upwards to take the oaths.*

That the Oaths in faid Act mentioned and thereby appointed to be taken in ftead of the Oaths of Allegiance and Supremacy, and each of them be and fhall be forthwith Adminiftred and given unto all Male perfons of the Age of Eighteen Years, or above, Inhabiting or Refiding in any Town or Place within this Province (that have not already taken the fame, and fhall make it fo appear) by his Excellency the Governour, or the Lieutenant, or Deputy Governour, or any two or more of the Council or Affiftants, or fuch others

as

# Allegiance to be Sworn 57

as shall be thereunto appointed by the Governour; and the List of the Names of all persons so Sworn, to be returned into the Secretary's Office.

## And be it further Enacted by the Authority aforesaid.

That if any person or persons shall refuse to take the said Oaths, or either of them, when tendered to him or them by any persons lawfully Authorized, as is aforesaid; to Administer or Tender the same; the person or persons so Tendering the said Oaths, or either of them, shall commit the said person and persons so refusing to the Common Goal, or House of Correction; there to remain without Bail, or Mainprize, for the space of Three Months; Unless such Offender shall pay down to the said person or persons so Tendring the said Oaths, or either of them, such Sum of Money, not exceeding Forty Shillings; as the said person or persons so Tendring the said Oaths, or either of them shall require such Offender to pay for his said refusal; which Money shall be paid to the Select-Men, or Overseers of the poor of the Town, or place where such Offender did last inhabit. *Penalty for refusing*

AND Unless every such Offender, shall also become bound, with two Sufficient Sureties, with Condition to be of the Good Behaviour; and also to appear at the next General Quarter Sessions of the Peace, to be held for the same County, where such Offender doth Inhabit or Reside; at which Court of Quarter Sessions, the said Oaths shall be again Tendered to every such Offender, by the Justices of the said Court in open Sessions. And if the said Offender, shall refuse to take the said Oaths or either of them, when Tendred to him by the said Justices in open Sessions as is aforesaid; the said Justices Tendring the said Oaths, shall Commit the said Person and Persons so refusing, to the Common Goal, or House of Correction, there to remain for the space of six Months, unless every such Offender shall pay down to the Justices so Tendring the said Oaths, such Sum of Money, not exceeding Ten Pounds, nor under Five Pounds, as the said Justices shall require such Offender to pay for his Second Refusal; the said Money to be disposed of in manner aforesaid; and unless every such Offender shall likewise become Bound with Two Sufficient Sureties, with Condition to be of the good Behaviour, until he or they do take the said Oaths.

And whereas there are certain persons who scruple the taking of any Oath.

## Be it Enacted by the Authority aforesaid

That every such Person shall Make and Subscribe the Declaration of Fidelity following, viz. I *A. B.* Do sincerely Promise, and solemnly Declare before God and the World; That I will be True and Faithful to King *WILLIAM*, and Queen *MARY*: And I do Solemnly Profess and Declare, that I from my Heart, Abhor, Detest, and Renounce as Impious and Heretical, that Damnable Doctrine and Position. That Princes Excommunited *Declaration of fidelity.*

cated or Deprived by the Pope, or any Authority of the SEE of ROME may be Deposed or Murdered by their Subjects, or any other whatsoever. And I do Declare that no Forreign Prince, Person, Prelate, State or Potentate hath, or ought to have any Power, Jurisdiction, Superiority, Preheminence or Authority, Ecclesiastical or Spiritual, within the Realm of *England*, or any of Their Majesties Dominions.

# An Act,
## For the Establishing of Form's of Oaths.

**Be** it Declared and Enacted, by the Governour, Council, and Representatives, in General Court Assembled. And by the Authority of the same.

That the several Forms of Oaths here under Written, **Be and are hereby Established,** To be Given and Administred unto the Respective Officers for whom they are appointed. As followeth,

**Counsellors Oath.**

YOU *A. B.* being Chosen, and Admitted of Their Majesties Council within this Their Province, do Swear by the Everliving God. That you will to the best of your Judgment at all times, freely give your Advice to the Governour, for the Good Management of the Publick Affairs of this Government; and that you will not directly nor indirectly Reveal such Matters as shall be Debated in Council, and Committed to your Secrecy. But will in all things be a True and Faithful Counsellor when you are thereunto Required. *So Help you God.*

**Justice of Peace Oath.**

YOU *A. B.* Swear, That as Justice of the Peace in the County of *S.* according to the Commission given you. You shall Dispense Justice Equally and Impartially in all Cases. And do Equal Right to the Poor and to the Rich, after your Cunning, Wit and Power, and according

# Forms of Oaths.

according to Law. And you shall not be of Council in any Quarrel that shall come before you: You shall not Let for Gift or other Cause, But well and truly you shall do your Office of Justice of the Peace in that behalf, Taking only appointed Fees. And you shall not direct or cause to be directed any Warrant (by you to be made) to the Parties; but you shall Direct your Warrant to the Sheriff, his Under-Sheriff or Deputy, Tything-men, or other Officers, proper for the Execution of the same in the County. And this you shall do without Favour or Respect to Persons. *So help you God.*

YOU Swear, That you will well and truly Serve the King and Queens Majesties, in the Office of the Sheriff of the County of *S.* And do the King and Queens profit in all things that belongeth to you to do by way of your Office, as far forth as you can or may, you shall truly keep the King and Queens Rights, and all that belongs to the Crown; you shall not Respite the King and Queens Debts for any Gift or Favour, where you may Raise them without great grievance of the Debtors; you shall truly and uprightly Treat the people of your Sheriffwick, and do Right as well to Poor as to Rich, in all that belongeth to your Office; You shall do no wrong to any man, for any Gift or other Behest or Promise of Goods, for Favour nor Hate; You shall disturb no mans Right, you shall truly Acquit at the Treasury, all those of whom you shall any thing receive of Their Majesties Debts; you shall nothing take whereby Their Majesties may lose, or whereby the Right may be Letted or disturbed, or Their Majesties Delayed; you shall truly return, and truly Serve all Their Majesties Writs, as far forth as shall be to your Cunning; you shall take no Bayliff into your Service, but such as you will Answer for, and of true and sufficient men in the County, & shall cause each of your Bayliffs, to make such Oath as you make your self in that belongeth to their Occupation. And over this in Eschewing and Restraint of the Man-flaughters, Robberies, and other manifold Grievous Offences that be done daily. All these things you shall truly observe and keep as *God help you*.

*Sheriff or Marshals Oath, Mutatis Mutandis.*

YOU as Foreman of this Inquest for the Body of this County of *S.* You shall diligently Enquire, and a true Presentment make of all such Matters and Things as shall be given you in Charge; The King and Queens Majesties Council, your Fellows and your own, you shall keep secret; You shall Present no man for Envy, Hatred or Malice; neither shall you leave any man Unpresented for Love, Fear, Favour or Affection, or hope of Reward; but you shall present things truly as they come to your knowledge, according to the best of your Understanding. *So help you God.*

*Grand Jurors Oath*

THE same Oath which you Foreman hath taken on his part, you and every of you on your behalf shall well and truly observe and keep. *So help you God.*

You

## Forms of Oaths

**Petit Jurors Oath.** YOU shall well and truly try and true deliverance make between Our Soveraign Lord and Lady, the King and Queen, and the Prisoners at the Bar, whom you shall have in Charge according to your Evidence. *So help you God.*

**Jurors Oath in civil Cases.** YOU Swear, That in all Causes betwixt Party and Party that shall be Committed unto you: You will give a true Verdict therein according to Law, and the Evidence given you. *So help you God.*

**Town Clerks Oath.** YOU Swear, That in the Office of Town Clerk within the Town of B. whereto you are Chosen: You will diligently and faithfully Attend & Discharge the Duty of your Place, & duly Observe the Directions of the Law in all things whereto your Office hath relation, and thereby Committed to your Care and Trust. *So help you God.*

**Oath of Leather Sealer Clerk of the Market, Culler of Fish, Packer, Gager,** *Mutatis Mutandis.* YOU Swear, That you will from time to time, diligently and faithfully Discharge and Execute the Office of within the Limits whereto you are Appointed for the Ensuing Year, and until another be Chosen in your place; and that in and by all the particulars mentioned in the Laws whereto your Office hath Relation; and that you will do therein Impartially according to Law, without Fear or Favour. *So help you God.*

**Constables Oath.** WHEREAS you *A. B.* are Chosen Constable within the Town of C. for One Year now following, and until other be Chosen and Sworn in your Place: You do Swear, That you will carefully Intend the Preservation of the Peace, the Discovery and preventing all Attempts against the same: That you will duly Execute all Warrants which shall be sent unto you from Lawful Authority; and faithfully Attend all such Directions in the Laws, and Orders of Court, as are, or shall be Committed to your Care. That you will faithfully and with what Speed you can, Collect and Levy all such Fines, Distresses, Rates, Assesments and Sums of Mony, for which you shall have sufficient Warrants according to Law; Rendring an Accompt thereof, and paying in the same according to the Direction in your Warrant. And with like faithfulness, Speed and Diligence will Serve all Writs, Executions, and Distresses in Private Causes betwixt Party and Party, and make Returns thereof duly into the same Court, where they are Returnable. And in all these things you shall deal seriously and faithfully whilst you shall be in Office without any Sinister Respects of Favour or Displeasure. *So help you God.*

An Act

## Forms of Writs & Processes

# An Act,

### For the Establishing of Presidents and Forms of Writts, and Processes.

**B**e it Enacted and Declared by the Governour Council and Representatives, in General Court assembled, And by the Authority of the same.

That the several Forms of Writts and Processes, here under Written; **Be and hereby are Established** to be the Forms to be observed by the Respective Officers that are or shall be appointed and Impowred to grant the same.

**W**ILLIAM and MARY by the Grace of God of *England, Scotland, France,* and *Ireland,* King and Queen; Defenders of the Faith, &c.

**T**O Our Sheriff or Marshal of Our County of Greeting.

**W**EE Command that upon Receipt hereof, You forthwith make out your Precepts, directed unto the Select-Men of each Respective Town within your Precinct, Requiring them to cause the Free-holders and other Inhabitants of their several Towns duly qualified as in and by our Royal Charter is directed; to Assemble at such time and place as they shall Appoint, to Elect and Depute one or more persons (being Freeholders within our said Province) according to the Number Set and Limited by an Act of our General Assembly within the same, to Serve for, and Represent them respectively, in a Great and General Court or Assembly by us appointed to be Convened, Held and Kept for our Service at the *Town-House* in *Boston,* upon            the         Day of            next Ensuing the Date of these Presents. And to cause the person or persons so Elected, and Deputed by the major part of the Electors present at such Election, to be timely Notified and Summoned by the Constable or Constables of such Town to attend our Service in the said Great and General Court or Assembly, on the Day above prefixed, by nine in the morning; and so *de Die in Diem,* during their Session and Sessions, and to Return the said Precepts, with the Names of the

*Writ for Calling an Assembly*

Persons

Persons so Elected and Deputed unto Your self. Whereof you are to make Return, together with this Writ, and of your Doings therein under your Hand into our Secretary's Office at *Boston*, one day at the least, before the said Courts Sitting. Hereof you may not Fail at your Peril. Witness Sir *W. P.* Knight, Our Captain General, and Governour in Chief in and over our Province of the *Massachusetts-Bay* in *New-England*. Given at *Boston*, under the Publick Seal of our Province aforesaid the          day of          169   In the          Year of our Reign.

By His Excellencies Command

Suffolk. ss

IN Observance of Their Majesties Writ to me directed. These are in Their Majesties Names to Will and Require you forthwith to cause the Freeholders and other Inhabitants of your Town, that have an Estate of Freehold in Land within this Province or Territory, of Forty Shillings *Per Annum* at the least, or other Estate to the value of Forty Pounds *Sterling*, to Assemble and meet at such time and place as you shall appoint; then and there to Elect and Depute one or more Persons (being Freeholders within the Province) according to the number set and Limited by an Act of the General Assembly, to serve for and Represent them in a Great and General Court or Assembly Appointed to be Convened, held and kept for Their Majesties Service at the *Town-House* in *Boston* upon the          day of          next          Ensuing the Date hereof; and to cause the person or persons so Elected and Deputed by the Major part of the Electors present at such Election; to be timely Notified and Summoned by one or more of the Constables of the Town; to attend Their Majesties Service in the said Great and General Court or Assembly; on the Day above prefixed, by Nine in the Morning; and so *De Die in Diem* during their Session and Sessions. Hereof Fail not, and make return of this Precept; with the Names of the person or persons so Elected and Deputed; with their being Summoned; unto my self on or before the          day of          abovesaid. Given under My Hand and Seal at          the          Day of          169   In the          Year of Their Majesties Reign.

To the Select-Men of the          A. B
Town of          Greeting          of the County of

Return

PUrsuant to the Precept within Written, the Freeholders and other Inhabitants of this Town Qualified as is therein directed, upon due Warning given, Assembled and met together the          Day of          and then did Elect and Depute, *A. B.* and *C. D.* to serve for and Represent them in the Session and Sessions of the Great and General Court or Assembly appointed to be begun and held at *Boston* on the          day of          the said persons being

## Forms of Writs & Processes 63

being Chosen by the major part of the Electors present at said Meeting. Dated in the           Day of

The Persons Chosen are
Notified thereof, and
Summoned to attend               } Select-Men.
accordingly. By me *A. B.*
Constable of *C.*

*Essex ss.*

TO the Sheriff or Marshal of the said County, or either of their Deputies or Constables of the Town of *S.* or to any or either of them. In Their Majesties Names, You are Required to Summon and give Notice unto *T. P.* of            ( if he may be found in your Precincts ) that he appear before me *J. H.* Esq; one of Their Majesties Justices of the Peace, for the County aforesaid, at my Dwelling House in *S* on           being the        day of          at          of the Clock in the Forenoon, then and there to Answer *E. L.*
        in a Plea of
        to the value of
        as shall then and there appear with all due Damages, making true Return as the Law directs. You are also hereby further Required to Signifie unto the said *T. P.*
That he may not Fail in the Premises, as he will Answer the Contempt at the Peril of the Law in this case made and provided.   Dated in the          day of          In the
Year of Their Majesties Reign.

*Summons for appearance before a justice.*

*Essex ss.*

TO the Sheriff or Marshal of the said County, or Constables of the Town of *S.* or to any, or either of them Greeting. Whereas *T. P.* of         Cooper, was Served with Summons, Granted by me, *J. H.* Esq; one of the Justices of the said County for his Appearance before me on         the          day of          past, to Answer *E. L.* of         Merchant, in a plea of
       to the value of           with due Damages, the said *T. P.* making Default in appearance. These are in Their Majesties Names, to Will and Require you therefore to take the Body of the said *T. P.* ( if he may be found in your Precinct ) and him safely keep, so that he may be had before me on          being the        day of         at          of the Clock in the Forenoon, as well to Answer the said *E. L.* of his Plea aforesaid, as for his Contempt, making true Return of this Writ, as the Law directs. Dated at the          day of          In the          Year of Their Majesties Reign.                    R.                         To

*Warrant for contempt.*

## Forms of Writs & Processes

**Attachment before a Justice of the Peace.**

Suffolk ss.

TO the Sheriff or Marshal of the said County, or either of their Deputies or Constables of the Town of *B.* or to any or either of them. In Their Majesties Names, You are Required to Attach the Goods or Estate of *J. N.* of *B.* to the value of          And for want thereof, you are to take the Body of the said *J. N.* (if he may be found in your Precincts) and him safely keep, so that he may be had before *J. E.* Esq; one of the Justices of the said County on          being the          day of          at          of the Clock in the Forenoon, to Answer *L. M.* of          in a Plea of          to the value of          as shall then and there appear, with all due Damages, making true Return of this Writ as the Law directs. Dated at *B* the          day of          in the          Year of Their Majesties Reign.

**Execution Granted by a Justice of Peace.**

Suffolk ss.

WILLIAM and MARY, &c. To the Sheriff or Marshal of our said County, his Deputy or Deputies, or Constables of the Town of          or to any or either of them. We Command you that without any delay, you Levy of the Money or Estate of *J. N.* of *B.*          (if it may be found in your Precincts,) the Sum of          with          Shillings more for this Writ, and deliver the same unto *L. M.* of          to Satisfie a Judgement obtained against the aforesaid *J. M.* for          with his Costs and Damages occasioned and accruing by a Suit Commenced against him before *J. E.* Esq; one of our Justices Assigned to keep our Peace in our said County the          day of          and in want of the said Money or other Estate of the said *L. M.* his Satisfaction. We Command you to take the Person of the said *J. N.*          and him Commit to the Custody of the Keeper of our Prison in *B.*          where he is to continue until the said Debt is satisfied, or that he be Discharged by the Creditor, or otherwise by Order of Law. Hereof fail not at your peril, making true Return of this our Writ as the Law directs. Witness our said Justice at          this          day of          In the          Year of our Reign

**Attachment to the Superiour or Inferiour Court.**

Suffolk ss.

WILLIAM and MARY &c. To the Sheriff or Marshal of our said County, or either of their Deputies Greeting, We command you to Attach the Goods or Estate of *D. T.* of          to the value of          and for want thereof to take the Body of the said *D. T.* (if he may be found in your Precinct) and          safely keep, so that you have before our Justices at our next          Court of          to be Holden at          within or for our said County on the          day of          next, then and there to Answer to *C. L.*          in an Action of          as shall then and there appear with Damages; and have you there this Writ. Witness *W. S.* Esq; At *B.* this          day of          In the Year of our Reign

## Forms of Writs & Processes 65

WILLIAM and MARY, &c. To A. B. of C.     *Summons,*
Greeting. We Command you, That you appear at our    *Appearance*
Court of    to be Held at B. for or within the County of S. *upon Goods*
on the    *Tuesday* in    next, to Answer unto C. D. of *Attached*
   in an Action of
to the value of
   which the said
C. D. hath Commenced to be then and there Heard and Determined,
to Respond which Action, your Goods or Estate are Attached to the
value of

Hereof fail not at your Peril. Witness W. S. Esq; At B. the
day of    In the Year of our Reign
                                              *J. W.*

WILLIAM and MARY &c. To our Sheriff or Marshal of our
County of E. or either of their Deputies Greeting: Whereas A.   *Writ of*
B. of C. Yeoman before our Justices of our    Court of    *Facias Ha-*
Held for, or within our said County of E. at S upon the    *bere Posseffi-*
Tuesday in N past, by the Consideration of our said Court, Recovered *onem and*
his Term yet to come of and in    Messuage or Tenement with the *Writ of*
Appurtenances, or    Acres of Land, Pasture or Meadow lying in *Fieri Facias*
the    of D. within your Precincts against E. F. of G. Carpenter, *for Dama-*
who had unjustly put out and Amoved the said A. B. from his Possef- *ges and*
sion thereof, and also there Recovered    Pounds    *Costs.*
and    Pence for Costs and Damages which he has Sustained by
reason of the said Offence and Ejectment, and Expended for the Removal thereof, as to us has been made to appear of Record. We Command you therefore that without delay you cause the said A B of and
in the aforesaid Tenement with the Appurtenances, or Land to have Possession of his Term yet to come. We also Command you, that of the
Goods, Chattels or Lands of the said E. F. within your Precinct at the
value thereof in Money, you cause the said A. B. to be paid and satisfied
the aforesaid Sum of    Pounds    Shillings &c.    Pence ; which to
the said A. B. in the said Court was adjudged for his Costs & Damages with
   Shillings more for this Writ, and thereof also to satisfie your Self
for your own Fees. And for want of such Goods, Chattels, or Land of the
said E. F's to be by him shewn unto you, or found within your Precinct to
satisfie the aforesaid Sums. We then Command you to take the Body of the
said E. F. and him Commit unto the Keeper of your Goal in S. within
our said Prison, whom we likewise Command to receive him the said
E. F. and him safely to keep, until he pay unto the said A. B. the full
Sum above-mentioned, and be by him Released, and also satisfie your Fees.
And this Writ with your doings, therein you are to Return unto our said
   Court of    to be Holden at S. upon the
*Tuesday* in N. next. Witness W. S. Esq; in S. the
day of    In the    Year of our Reign.
                                             *T. H.*

## Forms of Writs and Processes

**Execution.**

WILLIAM and MARY, &c. To our Sheriff or Marshal of our County of S. or either of their Deputies Greeting. Whereas *A. B.* of C.. Yeoman Recovered Judgment against *D. E.* of *F.* Carpenter before our Justices of our      Court      Holden for or within our said County of S. on the last *Tuesday* in      Moneth past, for the Sum of      Pounds      Shillings and      Pence in Money Debt or Damage, and      Pounds      Shillings and      Pence for Costs of Suit as to us appears of Record whereof Execution remains to be done. We Command you therefore, That of the Goods, Chattels or Lands of the said *D. E.* within your Precinct, you cause to be paid and satisfied, at the value thereof in Money the aforesaid Sum of      Pounds      Shillings and      Pence, with      Shillings more for this Writ, and thereof also to satisfie your self for your own Fees; and for want of such Goods, Chattels or Lands of the said *D. E*'s to be by him shewn unto you, or found within your Precinct to satisfie the aforesaid Sums. We Command you to take the Body of the said *D. E.* and him Commit unto the Keeper of our Goal in *B.* within the said Prison, whom we likewise Command to receive the said *D. E.* and him safely to keep, until he pay unto the said *A. B.* the full Sum above-mentioned, and be by him Released, and also satisfie your Fees, and this Writ with your doings therein you are to Return unto our said      Court      to be Holden at *B.* upon the last *Tuesday* in      Moneth next. Witness *J. R.* Esq; in *B.* the .      day of      169 In the Year of our Reign.

*J. W.*

**Scire Facias.**

WILLIAM and MARY &c. To our Sheriff or Marshal of our County of S. &c. Greeting. Whereas *C. D.* before our Justices of our      Court of      Holden for or within our said County of S      at *B*      the last Tuesday of      in the      Year of our Reign: By Consideration of our said Justices Recovered against *A. B.* of *B*      Yeoman      Pounds, Debt, or Damage, and also      Shillings for Costs and Charges by him about his Suit in that behalf, Expended whereof the said *C.D.* is Convict, as to us appears of Record, and although the Judgement be thereof Rendred, yet the Execution of the said Debt and Costs doth yet remain to be made, whereof the said *C. D.* hath Supplicated us to provide Remedy for him in that behalf. Now to the end, That Justice be done, We command you, that by honest and lawfull men of your Precinct, you make known to the said *C D* that he be before our Justices of our      Court of      to be Holden in or for our said County of S. at *B.* on the last Tuesday of      next, to shew cause (if any he have) wherefore the said *C. D.* ought not to have his Execution against him of the Debt and Cost aforesaid. And further

## Forms of Writs & Processes

...... to do and receive that which our said Court shall then Consider, ..... have there then the Names of them by whom to him you make ...... the same, and this Writ. Witness J. R. Esq; at B. the
          In the      Year of our Reign.
                                           J. W.

*...... ss.*

TO A. B. of C. In Their Majesties Names you are Required to make your Appearance before Their Majesties Justices of the next    Court of    to be Holden for or within the County aforesaid, at B upon the    *Tuesday* of Instant, to give Evidence of what you know Relating to a Plea or Action of        then and there to be Heard and Tryed betwixt R. S. Plaintiff, and S. T. Defendant. Hereof fail not as you will Answer your Default under the Pains and Penalty of the Law in that behalf made and provided. Dated in B the    day of In the    Year of Their Majesties Reign.

*Summons to give Evidences*

*S. folk ss.*

TO the Sheriff or Marshal of the said County, or Constables of the Town of M. or to any or either of them. In Their Majesties Names You are Required to Replevin one of T. P. now Distreined or Impounded by J. G. and deliver the said    unto the said T. P. Provided he give Bond to the value of    with sufficient Sureties or Sureties to Prosecute his Replevin at the next Inferiour Court of Pleas to be Holden for the said County at B on the last *Tuesday* of    and so from Court to Court until the Cause be Ended; and to pay such Costs and Damages as the said J. G. shall by Law Recover against him. Hereof fail not, and make true Return of this Writ, with your Doings therein as the Law Directs. Dated in B. the    day of    In the    Year of Their Majesties Reign.

*Replevin*

WILLIAM and MARY &c. To A. B. Greeting, Whereas in the Record and Process, and also in giving judgement, and Issuing Execution of a Suit which was before our Justices of our Inferiour Court of Pleas, Holden at B within the County of S on the    *Tuesday* of    last past, between C. D. Plaintiff, and F. G. Defendant of a Plea        Error, Manifest doth appear to have Intervened, to the grievous Damage of the said F. G. as of his Complaint We have received, We willing that        Error,

*Writ of Error.*

S

## Forms of Writs & Processes

Error, if any there be in this behalf, in due manner be Corrected, and speedy Justice according to the Law, to the Party aforesaid, therein be done as it becometh us. Command you, that if Judgement be thereon given, and Execution Issued, that the Record and Process of the Suit aforesaid and also the Execution thereon Issued, and all things touching the same in any manner, you have before our Justices of our Superiour Court of Judicature, at            in our said Province, the            next, under your Seal; so that our said Justices of our said Superiour Court may then and there have them, and the Process and Record aforesaid, and also the said Execution being inspected, may further therein do what of right ought to be done. Have with you then this Writ. Witness            At this            day of            In the            Year of our Reign

*Supersedeas*

WILLIAM and MARY, &c. To the Sheriff of our County of            Greeting, Whereas C. D lately in our            Court of            hath Recovered against F. G as well            Pounds Debt as his Damages, which by occasion of the Detaining of the said Debt to him in our said Court were adjudged, whereof he is Convict, as by the Record and Process of the Suit aforesaid, before our            Justices of the said            Court fully appears, as from the grievous Complaint of the said F. G We have received, and that in the Record and Process, and in Rendring of Judgement of the Suit aforesaid Error manifest hath Intervened to the grievous damage of the said F. G and we willing that Error therein, if any be, in due manner be Corrected, and to the said F. G full and speedy Justice in this behalf to be done: have Commanded the aforesaid            by our Writ, that if Judgement therein be given, he distinctly and aptly send the Record and Process of the Suit aforesaid, with all things touching the same unto            under his Seal, and that Writ, so that            may have            the            day of            next Ensuing; where that the Record and Process being inspected, we may cause further therein to be done as of right, and according to Law ought to be done. Nevertheless the Record and Process aforesaid, with all things touching the same before the aforesaid            day of            into our said            Court of            cannot conveniently be sent, and so Error therein, if any be, in the mean time, cannot be discussed, and therefore we Command you that if before the Receiving of that Writ you have not made Execution of this Judgement aforesaid then as well from further taking, Arresting, Imprisoning, Exacting, Outlawing, or in any thing molesting the aforesaid F. G on the occasion aforesaid, as of taking in Execution any Goods or Chattels, Lands or Tenements whatsoever of the said F. G by occasion of the Judgement aforesaid, until the Plea upon our Writ of Error to be corrected depending Undiscussed be fully determined, you altogether Supersede, and have with you then and there this Writ. Witness W. S. Esq; at B the            day of            In the Year of our Reign

# An Act,
## For Regulating Fees.

**B**e it Enacted and Ordained by the Governour, Council, and Representatives, Convened in General Court or Assembly. And it is hereby Enacted and Ordained by the Authority of the same.

That the Establishment of the Fees belonging to the several Offices in this Province; be as followeth.

### Justices Fees.

|  | l | s | d |
|---|---|---|---|
| For every Attachment or Summons for Actions not Exceeding Forty Shillings, Sixpence. | 00 | 00 | 6 |
| Sub-Pœna, each Witness, Two-Pence. | 00 |  | 2 |
| Entring the Action, Three Shillings. | 00 | 03 |  |
| Every Execution, Two Shillings. | 00 | 02 |  |
| Filing Papers, each Paper Two-pence | 00 |  | 2 |
| Every Warrant for Criminals, one Shilling. | 00 | 01 |  |
| Bond for Appeal, one Shilling. | 00 | 01 |  |
| Copy of Evidences, the least Six-pence. | 00 | 00 | 6 |
| Copy of a Judgment, Six-pence. | 00 | 00 | 6 |
| Every Recognizance, Two Shillings. | 00 | 02 |  |
| Confessing Judgment, one Shilling. | 00 | 01 |  |
| Affidavit out of Court, | 00 | 01 |  |
| Each Dayes attendance at the Sessions, to be paid out of the Fines, Four Shillings. | 00 | 04 |  |
| Acknowledging of a Deed or Mortgage or any other Instrument, | 00 | 02 |  |

Coro-

## Coroners Fees.

|  | l | s | d |
|---|---|---|---|
| For taking every Inquisition, to be paid out of the Estate of the deceased Thirteen Shillings and Four pence. | 00 | 13 | 04 |
| If no Estate, then to be paid by the County Treasurer, Six Shillings and Eight-Pence. | 00 | 06 | 08 |

## Fees for Probate of Wills, granting Administrations. &c.

|  | l | s | d |
|---|---|---|---|
| For granting Administration, Bond and Letter of Administration, under the Seal of the Office, if the Inventory amount to Thirty pounds or upwards, to the Judge Four Shillings, to the Register Three Shillings, Six-pence, | 00 | 07 | 06 |
| If the Inventory be under Thirty Pounds, Five Shillings. | 00 | 05 | 00 |
| Probate of a Will where the Inventory amounts to Thirty Pounds or upwards; to the Judge Three Shillings and Sixpence to the Register Two Shillings and Sixpence. | 00 | 06 | 00 |
| If under Thirty Pounds, Four Shillings | 00 | 04 | 00 |
| Recording a Will or Inventory of one page, & Filing the same, Two Shillings and Sixpence | 00 | 02 | 06 |
| If more, each page of Twenty eight lines eight words in a line, one Shilling. | 00 | 01 | 00 |
| For a Copy of a Will or Inventory, Twelve pence a page, each page to contain as aforesaid. | 00 | 01 | 00 |
| Allowing Accompts, Settling and Dividing of Intestate, Estates, Five Shillings. | 00 | 05 | 00 |

Every

# Regulating of Fees

|  | l | s | d |
|---|---|---|---|
| Every Citation, One Shilling | 00 | 01 | 00 |
| Every Quietus, Four Shillings | 00 | 04 | 00 |
| Warrant for Apprizement, Two Shillings | 00 | 02 | 00 |
| Making out a Commission to receive and Examin the Claims of Creditors to Insolvent Estates and Registring of the same, Three Shillings | 00 | 03 | 00 |
| Registring of the Commissioners Report after the Rate of One Shilling *Per Page*, to be accounted as aforesaid. | | | |
| For Entring an Order upon the Administrator to pay out the Estate in proportion unto the several Creditors Returned by the Commissioners, One Shilling and Six-pence. | 00 | 01 | 06 |

## Secretarys Fees

|  | l | s | d |
|---|---|---|---|
| For Engrossing the Acts or Laws of the General Assembly, Ten Shillings each, to be paid out of the Publick Revenue | 00 | 10 | 00 |
| Every Commission for the Justices of each County, and Comission of Oyer and Terminer Ten Shillings, to be paid out of the Publick Revenue | 00 | 10 | 00 |
| Every Commission for a Military Officer, Three Shillings, to be paid out of the Publick Revenue | 00 | 03 | 00 |
| Special Warrant or Mittimus by Order of the Governour and Council, each Two Shillings & Six-pence. | 00 | 02 | 06 |
| Every Commission under the Great Seal for Places of Profit, Ten Shillings | 00 | 10 | 00 |
| Every Bond Two Shillings | 00 | 02 | 00 |
| Every Order of Council to the benefit of particular persons, Two Shillings and Six-pence. | 00 | 02 | 06 |
| Every Petition to the Governour and Council or General Assembly according to the Import from two shillings and Six-pence to Ten Shillings | | | |
| A Pass or Sea Brief, Three Shillings | 00 | 03 | 00 |
| A Bill of Health, Three Shillings | 00 | 03 | 00 |
| Every Writ for Electing of Assembly-Men directed to the Sheriff or Marshal, under the Province Seal, Five Shillings, to be paid out of the Publick Revenue. | 00 | 05 | 00 |

T For

## Regulating Fees

|  | l | s | d |
|---|---|---|---|
| For Transcribing the Acts or Laws passed by the General Assembly into a Book, Twelve-pence a Page, each page to contain Twenty Eight Lines, Eight Words in a Line, and so proportionably, to be paid out of the Publick Revenue. | | | |

## In the Superiour Court

### The Justices Fees.

|  | l | s | d |
|---|---|---|---|
| Entry of every Action for Tryal, Twelve Shillings. | 00 | 12 | 00 |
| out of which to the Clerk, Two Shillings. | 00 | 02 | 00 |
| Taking every Special Bayl, Two Shillings. | 00 | 02 | 00 |
| Allowing of a Writ of Error, Three Shillings | 00 | 03 | 00 |
| Allowing a *Habeas Corpus*, Two Shillings. | 00 | 02 | 00 |
| Confessing Judgement, Two Shillings. | 00 | 02 | 00 |
| Acknowledging Satisfaction of a Judgment on Record one Shilling | 00 | 01 | 00 |
| In all Criminal Cases where a Fine is set, Six Shillings | 00 | 06 | 00 |
| Taxing every Bill of Cost, One Shilling | 00 | 01 | 00 |

### Clerks Fees.

|  | l | s | d |
|---|---|---|---|
| Every Writ and the Seal, One Shilling and Six-pence. | 00 | 01 | 06 |
| Every Rule of Court, Six-pence | | | 06 |
| Filing every Declaration, One Shilling | 00 | 01 | 00 |
| To the Jury to be paid down by the Plaintiff, Six Shillings Sixpence | 00 | 06 | 06 |
| Entring Appearance, Six-pence | | | 06 |
| Signing a Judgement by Default, One Shilling | 00 | 01 | 00 |
| Taking every Verdict and Recording it, One Shilling | 00 | 01 | 00 |
| Copies of all Records, Twelve-pence a page, each page containing Twenty Eight Lines eight words in a Line. | 00 | 01 | 00 |
| Less then One Page, One Shilling. | | | |
| Every Action withdrawn non Suit, One Shilling. | 00 | 01 | 00 |
| Every Petition Read, One Shilling. | 00 | 01 | 00 |
| Order thereon One Shilling | 00 | 01 | 00 |
| Filing the Records of each Action, Two-pence a Paper | 00 | 03 | 00 |
| Every Execution, Two Shillings | 00 | 02 | 00 |

### In Criminal Cases

|  | l | s | d |
|---|---|---|---|
| Drawing and Ingrossing every Indictment or Information, Two Shillings | 00 | 02 | 00 |

Every

## Regulating Fees

|  | s | d |
|---|---|---|
| Every Appearance Six-pence. | 00 | 06 |
| For the Discharge of any person upon Bail for the peace, good behaviour, Contempt and the like and Warrant thereon, One Shilling. | 01 | 00 |
| For Awarding and making forth Process against the Defendant on Information, One Shilling | 01 | 00 |
| Every Warrant for the peace, or good behaviour One Shilling | 01 | 00 |

### In the Inferiour Court

#### Justices Fees.

| | s | d |
|---|---|---|
| Entry of every Action, Ten Shillings. | 10 | 00 |
| Of which the Clerk is to have Two Shillings | 02 | 00 |
| Taking Special Bail Two Shillings | 01 | 00 |
| Confessing Judgment One Shilling of which the Clerk one Quarter | | |
| Acknowledging Satisfaction of Judgment on Record, One Shilling | 01 | 00 |
| Taxing every Bill of Cost, One Shilling | 01 | 00 |
| whereof Six-pence to the Clerk | 00 | 06 |
| To the Jury to be paid down by the Plaintiff, Six Shillings Six-pence. | 06 | 06 |

#### Clerks Fees

| | s | d |
|---|---|---|
| For every Writ and Seal, One Shilling. | 01 | 00 |
| Entring Appearance six-pence | 00 | 06 |
| Entring and Recording the Verdict, One Shilling. | 01 | 00 |
| Making up the Record, One Shilling | 01 | 00 |
| Copys of all Records Twelve Pence each page as before | 12 | 00 |
| Every Action withdrawn or Non-Suit, one shilling | 01 | 00 |
| Every Execution Two shillings. | 02 | 00 |

#### Clerk of the Sessions or Peace, his Fees.

| | s | d |
|---|---|---|
| Entring Complaint or Indictment, Two shillings | 02 | 00 |
| Discharge of a Recognizance, One Shilling | 01 | 00 |
| Making forth Process against Criminals, One shilling | 01 | 00 |
| Every Summons Three-pence. | 00 | 03 |
| Every Warrant for the Peace, or good Behaviour, one shilling | 01 | 00 |
| Every Licence for Houses of Publick Entertainment or Retailing, Five shillings | 04 | 00 |
| whereof two to the Clerk | 02 | 00 |

## Sheriff or Marshals Fees

### or Constables.

|  | l | s | d |
|---|---|---|---|
| For Serving every Summons for Tryal, one shilling | 00 | 01 | 00 |
| Every Capias or Attachment, Two shillings | 00 | 02 | 00 |
| And if above one Mile, three-pence *per* Mile besides | | | |
| Bayl Bond, One Shilling. | 00 | 01 | 00 |
| Levying Execution, for the first Twenty Pound or under, One shilling *Per* Pound, above that, not Exceeding Forty Pound, six-pence *per* Pound | | | |
| Above Forty Pound, not exceeding One Hundred Pound Three-pence *per* Pound, for whatsoever it exceeds One Hundred Pound, Two-pence *per* Pound. | | | |
| Besides Four-pence *per* Mile for Travel from Home. | | | |
| Every Tryal, One shilling | 00 | 01 | 00 |
| Every Precept for Choosing of Representatives Two Shillings, to be paid out of the County Assessment. | 00 | 02 | 00 |

### Cryers Fees.

|  | l | s | d |
|---|---|---|---|
| For calling of the Jury, six-pence. | 00 | 00 | 06 |
| Every Non Suit, Twelve-pence | 00 | 01 | 00 |
| Every Verdict, Twelve-pence. | 00 | 01 | 00 |

### Goalers Fees.

|  | l | s | d |
|---|---|---|---|
| For Turning of the Key upon every Prisoner Committed five shillings, *viz.* Commitment 2s. 6d. Discharge 2s 6d. | 00 | 05 | 00 |
| for Diet for each Prisoner, Two Shillings and six-pence *per* week, and so proportionable, he finding the same. | 00 | 02 | 06 |

### And be it further Enacted by the Authority of the same.

That what Officer soever shall ask, demand and take any greater or other Fee's than are beforementioned for the matters aforesaid, or any of them, and be thereof duly Convicted in any Court of Record within this Province, shall forfeit and pay the sum of Ten Pounds currant Money, One Moiety whereof to be unto Our Sovereign Lord and Lady the King and Queen, Their Heirs and Successors for and towards the Support of the Government of this Their Province, and the contingent charges thereof; And the other Moiety unto

the

the Informer or him that shall sue for the same in any Court of Record; wherein no Essoign, protection, or wager of law shall be allowed. And shall further pay unto the party grieved, double the value of the excessive Fees so taken.

# An Act,

For Ascertaining the number, and Regulating the House of Representatives.

**W**Hereas Their Majesties have been Graciously pleased by Their Royal Charter, to grant power unto the Great and General Court or Assembly of Their Province of the *Massachusetts-Bay*; from time to time to direct, appoint, and declare, what number of Representatives each County, Town or place shall Elect and Depute to serve for and Represent them Respectively, in the said Assembly.

**Be it therefore Enacted and Ordained by His Excellency the Governour, Council and Representatives, now in General Court Assembled, And by the Authority of the same:**

That henceforth every Town within this Province, consisting of the Number of Forty Freeholders, and other Inhabitants qualified by Charter to Elect shall and hereby are Injoyned to Choose and send one Freeholder as their Representative; and every Town consisting of the Number of one Hundred & Twenty Freeholders and other Inhabitants, qualified as aforesaid, or upwards may send Two such Representatives, and each Town of the number of Thirty Freeholders, and other Inhabitants qualified as aforesaid, or upwards, under Forty, are at liberty to send, or not; but may Choose and send one Representative, if they think fit, to serve for and Represent them Respectively in every Session of the Great and General Court or Assembly from time to time. And all Towns under Thirty Freeholders may send one to Represent them, or Joyn with the next Town in the Choice of their Representatives, they paying a proportionable part of the Charge. And no Town, shall at any time send more than Two Representatives, except *Boston*, who are hereby granted to choose and send Four.

V And

### Regulating the House of Representatives

**And be it further Enacted by the Authority aforesaid.**

That when and so often as His Excellency the Governour shall see cause to Convene and Hold a Great and General Court or Assembly, Writts shall Issue out from the Secretarys Office under the Seal of the Province, and Signed by the Governour, Thirty days at least, before the time appointed for such Assemblys meeting, directed unto the Sheriffs of the several Counties. And where there is no Sheriff in any County or place, there to be directed to the Marshall, commanding each of them respectively to send his Precepts to the Select men of the several and respective Towns within such County, to Assemble and call together the Freeholders and other Inhabitants qualified as aforesaid, to Choose and Elect one or more Freeholders, as the number in each Town is more or less, as above, to serve for and Represent them in such Great and General Court or Assembly : The major part of the Select-men in each Town respectively, to be present at such Meeting, and to give Directions for the regular and orderly Carrying on of the same : Who are to Return the said Precept, with the Names of such as shall be Chosen by the major part of the Electors present at such Meeting, under their Hands unto the Respective Sheriffs or Marshals, by them to be returned into the Secretary's Office, one day, at the least, before the time prefixed for the said Court or Assemblies Sitting.

**And it is further Enacted by the Authority aforesaid**

That the Representatives Assembled in any Great and General Court, shall be the Sole Judges of the Elections and Qualifications of their own Members; and may from time to time Settle, Order and Purge their House, and make such necessary Orders for the due Regulation thereof, as they shall see occasion. And Forty Representatives at any time so Assembled, shall be accounted a Number sufficient to Constitute a House, Pass Bills, and to Transact and Do Business proper to be done in that House; and such Acts to be esteemed valid and of Effect.

**And it is further Enacted by the Authority aforesaid**

That each Town respectively shall pay unto their several Representatives, during their Attendance on the Court, and for the necessary Time Expended in their Journeying to and from thence; Three Shillings in Money *Per Diem* within one Moneth next after the end of each Session Commencing from his Excellencies Arrival.

And

### Regulating the House of Representatives

#### And it is further Enacted by the Authority aforesaid

That every person Chosen to Serve for, and Represent any Town in the General Assembly, and accepting thereof, shall give his constant Attendance, during their Sessions, on pain of Forfeiting the Sum of Five Shillings *Per Diem* for his Neglect (without just Excuse made and allowed of by the House of Representatives) to be paid unto the Clerk of the said House, and is to be disposed of and Imployed as the House shall Direct; and in default of payment, to be Levied by Distress upon such Delinquents Goods, by Warrant from the said Clerk, by Order of the House, directed to the Sheriff of the County, his Under-Sheriff or Deputy, or Constable of the Town where such Representative Dwells: And no Representative shall depart or absent himself from the General Assembly, until the same be fully Finished, Adjourned or Prorogued, without the Licence of the Speaker and Representetives Assembled, to be Entred upon Record in the Clerks Book, on pain to every one so Departing or Absenting himself in any other manner, to lose his Wages. And the Inhabitants of such Town for which he Serves, shall be clearly Discharged of the said Wages against such person and his Executors for ever.

#### And further it is Enacted by the authority aforesaid

That no Member of the General Assembly, or his Servant during the time of their Sessions, or going to and from thence shall be Arrested, Sued, Imprisoned, or any ways molested or troubled or Compelled to make answer to any Suit, Bill, Plaint or Declaration, or otherwise: Cases of High Treason and Felony Excepted.

AN

# An Act,

For the preventing of Danger by the French Refiding within this Province.

There having been frequent Complaints made to this Court, That altho' feveral *French* Proteftants who lately fled from Perfecution; Came Over-Sea into this Province, and were Charitably Entertained and Succoured here; yet fince that, many of a Contrary Religion and Intereft, have been brought hither; and others have Obtruded themfelves; which (efpecially in this time of War, between the Two Crowns of *Enlgand* and *France*) proves a grievous Inconvenience; and the publick fafety is endangered, by fuffering fuch a mixt Company among us.

### For Remedy Whereof,

It is Enacted and Ordained by the Governour, Council, and Reprefentatives, Convened in General Affembly; and by the authority of the fame.

That from and after the Second Day of *January* next Enfuing; none of the *French* Nation be permitted to refide or be in any of the Sea-Port or Frontier Towns within this Province; but fuch as fhall be Licenfed by the Governour and Council. Nor fhall any of faid Nation open Shop, or Exercife any Manual Trade in any of the Towns of this Province; without the Approbation of the Select-Men, firft orderly obtained in Writing under their hands, on pain of Imprifonment.

And any Two Juftices of the Peace *Querum Unus*, within their Refpective Precincts, are hereby Impowred to Commit to Prifon any Perfon or Perfons Legally Convicted of Offending againft this Act; upon the Complaint of the Select-Men in any Town, or any Two of Them; and to remain in Prifon until Releafed by Order of the Governour and Council.

An Act

# Witchcraft

# An Act,

Against Conjuration, Witchcraft, and Dealing with Evil and Wicked Spirits.

FOR more particular Direction in the Execution of the Law against Witchcraft.

BE it Enacted by the Governour, Council, and Representatives in General Court Assembled, And by the Authority of the same.

That if any person or persons shall use, practise or Exercise any Invocation or Conjuration of any Evil and wicked Spirit, or shall Consult, Covenant with, Entertain, Employ, Feed or Reward any Evil and Wicked Spirit to or for any intent or purpose, or take up any Dead Man, Woman or Child, out of his, her, or their Grave, or any other Place where the Dead Body Resteth, or the Skin, Bone, or any other part of any Dead Person to be Employed or used in any manner of Witchcraft, Sorcery, Charm or Inchantment, or shall Use, Practice or Exercise any Witchcraft, Inchantment, Charm or Sorcery, whereby any person shall be Killed, Destroyed, Wasted, Consumed, Pined or Lamed in his or her Body, or any part thereof: That then every such Offender or Offenders, their Aiders, Abetters, and Counsellors, being of any of the said Offences duly and lawfully Convicted and Attainted, shall suffer pains of Death, as a Felon or Felons.

And further to the intent that all manner of Practice, Use or Exercise of Witchcraft, Inchantment, Charm or Sorcery, should be henceforth utterly avoided, abolished, and taken away.

Be it Enacted by the authority aforesaid

That if any person or persons shall take upon him or them by Witchcraft, Inchantment, Charm or Sorcery to tell or declare in what place any Treasure of Gold or Silver should or might be found or had in the Earth, or other secret places ; Or where Goods or Things Lost or Stolen should be found or become ; Or to the intent to provoke any person to unlawful Love, Or whereby any Cattel or Goods of any person shall be Destroyed, Wasted or Impaired, Or to hurt or destroy any person in his or her Body, although the same be not effected and done : That then all and every such person and persons so offending, and being thereof lawfully Convicted, shall for the said Offence suffer Imprisonment by the space of one whole Year, without Bail or Mainprize, and once in

every

## Regulation of the Assessment

every Quarter of the said Year, shall in some Shire Town, stand openly upon the Pillory by the space of six hours, and there shall openly confess his or her Error and Offence, which said Offence shall be written in Capital Letters, and placed upon the Breast of said Offender.

And if any person or persons being once Convicted of the same Offence, and shall again Commit the like Offence, and being of any of the said Offences the second time lawfully and duly Convicted and Attainted as is aforesaid, shall suffer pains of Death, as a Felon or Felons.

# An Act,

## For Regulating the former Assesment, and for Granting an Additional Supply of Money.

**W**HEREAS by an Act of this Assembly, made at their First Sessions, begun the Eighth Day of *June* last past, Entituled, *An Act for the Granting unto Their Majesties an Assessment upon Polls and Estates*.) There was Granted unto Their Majesties for the Defence of their Subjects and Interests, and for Prosecution of the War against the *French* and *Indian* Enemy, and the Defraying of other Publick Charges of the Province, a Rate or Tax of Ten Shillings Per Poll of all Male Persons of Sixteen Years and upwards, and a quarter part of one years value, or Income of all Estates Real and Personal, to be Assessed and Levied in manner as in and by the said Act is Directed.

And forasmuch as it appears, That in prosecution thereof, the Rules therein given have not been fully understood, or at least not attended which has occasioned an Inequality, and the Sum thereupon returned, to fall greatly short of what was expected, and of answering the necessity of the Publick Occasions. Therefore to the Intent that there may be a Regulation of the said Tax, and a further Supply made for their Majesties Service, to the ends before mentioned.

**B**e it Ordained and Enacted by the Governour, Council and Representatives in General Court Assembled, and by the Authority of the same,

That there be Five Commissioners appointed by this Court, for each

## Regulation of the Assessment

each County within the Province, to pass into the several Towns, lying within such County, at or before the Twenty Second day of *February* next coming; Who, together with the Select-men and Commissioner of each Town respectively, that made the Lists of said Assessment shall Review the same; which the said Select-men and Town Commissioners shall then Exhibit and Expose in the particulars thereof, both of Polls and Estate within such Town, with an Addition of all Polls and Estate which were before omitted, as well Noting the Names of all persons whom through Age and Infirmity, they expect should be exempted from the Poll Tax, as others. And the said Select-men, Town and County Commissioners, shall Regulate, Correct and Perfect such Lists according to the Rules herein after mentioned; setting down the Sums both for Heads and Estate in distinct Columns; *That is to say*, each Male Person of sixteen Years old and upwards, (except such as are by Law excepted) at Ten Shillings by the Poll, and all Houses, Warehouses, Tan-Yards, Orchards, Pastures, Meadows and Lands, Mills, Cranes and Wharfs, to be Estimated at seven years Income, as they are or may be Let for in the respective places where they lye; which seven years Income is to be Esteemed and Reputed the value of such Estate upon said Tax, and each Hundred Pound in value to be Rated Thirty Shillings thereof; Cattle to be valued as follows: *To wit*, each Ox and Horse kind of four years old or upwards, at Forty Shillings; each Cow of three years old or upwards, at Thirty Shillings; all Sheep and Swine of one year old or upwards, at Four Pound per Score. All Shipping, Goods, Wares, Merchandizes and Trading Stock and Estate by the Rule of common Estimation at the best discretion of the Assessors. Every Handicrafts-man for his Income at discretion aforesaid. Every Male Slave of Sixteen Years Old or upwards, at Twenty Pounds Estate. All which particulars of Estate aforesaid, as well Real as Personal, shall be Assessed to said Tax, Thirty Shillings for each Hundred Pound in value; and so proportionably; and where any Farmer or Occupier of Housing or Lands lying within any Town or Precinct, shall be hereafter Assessed to any Publick Tax of the Province for such Housing and Lands in his Occupation, the Landlord shall Reimburse unto said Farmer or Occupier such Sum and Sums of Mony as he shall pay for the same, where no particular Contract is made to the contrary.

Provided nevertheless, where the Treasurer shall Order payment to any place within such Respective Town or Neighbourhood,

## And further it is Enacted by the authority aforesaid,

That every person who shall Refuse or Neglect to render and give in to the Select-Men a particular Account of his Estate, shall be Assessed as aforesaid at discretion; and every person who shall give in a partial account shall be alike Assessed for so much as he leaves out; and if any Person find himself

## Regulation of the Assessment

self agrieved at any sum or sums that shall be set upon him by the Assessors, he may make application unto them for relief; and if he be not thereby eased, may further apply unto the Justices of such County at the next Quarter Sessions, and making it appear to them that he is over rated, they shall order an abatement accordingly.

### And it is further Enacted by the Authority aforesaid

That the Lists of the Respective Towns being Examined, Regulated, and Perfected as aforesaid; and Signed by the Select men, and Town Commissioner, shall be delivered unto the Commissioners for such County, and by them brought to *Boston* upon the First Wednesday in *March* next where the Commissioners for each County or the Major part of them, then and there met shall be a Committee to take an account of the sum total of each List, and if the whole shall not amount to the sum of Thirty Thousand Pounds (including the Sum already returned unto the Treasurer, for which his Warrants are gone forth) then the said Committee are hereby Impowred to make a further addition upon each Town Proportionably to what shall be wanting to make up Thirty Thousand Pounds in the whole, including as aforesaid. And if it appear unto the said Committee that any Town or County shall have been generally defective in not attending the Rules and Directions herein before given for the said Tax; then they are to Report the same unto the General Assembly at their next sitting to be Rectified and adjusted; but shall forthwith deliver the said Lists with the additional Sums, made to the same, unto the Treasurer, who is hereby Ordered and Impowred upon receipt thereof to Issue forth his Warrants affixed to said Lists and directed to the Constables or Collectors for each Town Respectively, for the Collecting and Levying of the same which is hereby granted to be paid in Money or otherwise to the Treasurers Satisfaction, unto the Treasurer, his Deputy or Deputys. And for manner and time as follows: That is to say,

Ten Thousand Pounds part of said Sum (besides what the Treasurers Warrants are already out for) at or before the First day of *May* next; and the full remainder of said Sum to make up the Thirty Thousand Pound as aforesaid; at or before the last day of *February*, which will be in the Year of Our Lord One Thousand Six Hundred Ninety Three; or

Provided nevertheless, where the Treasurer shall Order payment to particular persons within their Respective Towns or Neighbourhood, for Wages, or any other Disbursements due, in such case payment to be made in Merchantable Grain, Provisions or Cloathing, each at the currant Money Price.

### And it is further Enacted by the authority aforesaid

That the Commissioners for the several Counties for the ends within mentioned, be, as hereafter named, That is to say, For *Suffolk* Captain *Pen Townsend*, and Mr. *Timothy Tilestone*: For *Essex*, Captain *Samuel Gard-*

## Regulation of the Assessment

*ner*, and Mr. *Nehemiah Jewet*: For *Middlesex*, Major *Thomas Henchman*, and Mr. *Matthew Johnson*: For *Plimouth*, Captain *Nathaniel Thomas*, and Mr. *Samuel Clap*: For *Barnstable*, Captain *Thomas Tupper*, and Mr. *John Otis*: For *Bristol*, Captain *John Brown*, and Mr. *Samuel Peck*: For *Hampshire*, Captain *Samuel Partrig*, and Mr. *Joseph Hawley*: For *Yorkshire*, Mr. *John Wheelwright*, and Mr. *James Emery*: For *Martha's Vineyard* and *Nantucket*, Captain *John Gardner*, and Mr. *Joseph Norton*. And if any Select-men or Assessors, or Town Commissioner, shall willfully neglect or refuse to perform their Duty in the due and speedy Execution of this present Act, and be thereof Convict upon Information and Prosecution before the Justices in Quarter Sessions within the County whereto such person belongs; the said Court may impose upon such person or persons so refusing, or neglecting any Fine, not exceeding Five Pounds for any Offence; the same to be Levied and paid in to the Treasurer for the Use of Their Majesties, towards the Support of the Government of the Province, and Incident Charges thereof.

### And it is further Enacted

That the Select-men and Assessors in each Town, be, and hereby are Impowred (if they think fit) to Nominate and Appoint one or more able and sufficient persons within the Bounds and Limits of such Town, to be Collectors of the Money due to Their Majesties by this Act; for whose paying unto the Treasurer, his Deputy or Deputies, such Money as they shall be Charged withal, the Town by whom they are so Imployed, shall be Answerable.

### And it is further Enacted

That if any Constable or Collector shall be Remiss and Negligent of his Duty in not Levying and Paying unto the Treasurer, his Deputy or Deputies, such Sum and Sums of Money, as from time to time he shall have received, and as ought by him to have been paid within the respective times Set and Limited by the Warrant, or Estreat to him Committed, pursuant to the Acts of this Assembly, referring to said Tax, and is not paid, by reason of his failing in doing his Duty according to the Directions and Command therein: The Treasurer is hereby Impowred by Warrant under his Hand and Seal, after the Expiration of the time so set, to Levy all such Sum and Sums of Mony by Distress and Sale of such Defective Constable or Collectors Goods and Chattels, returning the Overplus (if any be), and for want of such Distress, to Commit the Offender to the Common Goal of the County.

### Be it Further Enacted

That if any Person, or Persons, shall refuse to pay the Several Sum and Sums, and Proportions, as have been, or shall be Further Assessed upon him or them, to pay in persuance of this or the Former Act Relating to Said Tax

**Constable or Collectors Power to Distrein**

Tax, or Assessment upon Demand made by the Constable or Collector of the Town, place or precinct, according to the precept of Estreats to him delivered. It shall and may be lawful to and for such Constable, or Collector, who are hereby thereunto Authorized, and Required for Nonpayment thereof, to Distrein the Person, or Persons so refusing, by his or their Goods or Chattels, and the Distress, or Distresses, so taken to keep by the Space of Four Dayes at the Cost and Charges of the Owner thereof. And if the said Owner do not pay the Sum and Sums of money so assessed upon him, within the said four dayes, then the said Distress or Distresses to be apprized by two, or three of the Inhabitants where the Distress is taken, and to be sold by the said Officer for payment of the said mony, and the Overplus coming by the said Sale (if any be) over and above the Charges of taking and keeping the said Distress or Distresses to be immediately restored to the Owner. And if any person or persons Assessed as aforesaid, shall refuse, or neglect to pay the sum or sums so assessed, by the Space of Twenty Dayes after demand thereof, where no sufficient Distress can or may be found, whereby the same may be Levied, in every

**For want of Distress to Commit the Person.**

such Case, two or more of the Select-men or Assessors in such Town, are hereby Authorized, by Warrant under their Hands and Seals to Commit such person or persons to the Common Goal, there to be kept without Bail or Mainprize until payment shall be made.

### And it is further Enacted

**Provision in case of persons Removal**

That where any Person or Persons have removed, or shall remove from any Town or place where he or they lived or had their residence at the time of makeing the Lists, of any Tax or Assessment, not having before paid the respective Sums or Proportion set upon them by said Tax, it shall and may be lawful, to and for the Constable or Collector, to whom any such Tax or Assessment is committed, with Warrant to Collect, who are hereby Authorized and Impowred to demand the sum or sums Assessed upon such person and persons, in what Town or place soever he or they may be found; and upon refusal or neglect to pay the same, to Distrein the said person or persons by his or their Goods and Chattels as aforesaid. And for want of such Distress, to Commit the party to the Common Goal, there to remain until payment be made.

**And for a present Supply** of Moneys to carry on the Publick Occasions of the Government, for the ends within mentioned.

### It is further Enacted and Ordained by the authority aforesaid

That the Governour and Council may, and hereby are Impowred to Borrow, and take up upon Loan of any person or persons any sum and sums of money, not Exceeding Five Thousand Pounds upon the Credit of this Act, and to make over and give for Security unto the person and

## Habeas Corpus Act

and persons so Lending, the one Third Part of the Moneys granted and to be Collected by virtue of the same, for the Repayment of the Moneys that shall be lent; with Interest for Forbearance after the Rate of Seven *Per Cent. Per Annum*; the said Interest Money to be paid at the end of every Three Months until repayment of the Principal.

AND WHEREAS much of the Arrears of the Rates and Assessments which were granted as a Fund for the Bills of Credit Emitted by the Late Government of the *Massachusetts Colony*, have been and are daily bringing into Their Majesties Treasury of this their Province, and Imployed in Payment of the Publick debts thereof, there being but few of those Bills now flying out, except what were borrowed by the present Government. **It is therefore Enacted,**

*Bills of Credit made currant in Publick Payments.*

That all the said Bills, as well those not Endors't, as others, shall be received in payment of all Taxes, or Assessments, and other Publick Payments whatsoever at Five Pound *per Centum* advance; any Act or Law to the contrary notwithstanding. And that those that have lent their Bills to the Treasury, shall have the same allowance of Five Pound *Per Centum*; for so much as shall be repaid them by discount, *Bona Fide* on their own account, with the Treasurer, for Rates, Impost, or Excise.

# An Act,

For the better Securing the Liberty of the Subject, and for prevention of Illegal Imprisonment.

**F**OR the speedy Relief of all Persons Imprisoned for Criminal, or supposed Criminal Matters, in such Cases where by Law they are Bailable.

**B**e it Enacted by the Governour, Council, and Representatives in General Assembly Convened, and it is Enacted by the Authority of the same

That whensoever any person or persons shall bring any *Habeas Corpus* directed

## Habeas Corpus Act

*Writs of Habeas Corpus within three dayes after service to be returned and the body broughts, if within 20 miles &c.*

Directed unto any Sheriff, or Sheriffs, Goaler, Minister or other person whatsoever, for any person in his or their Custody; and the said Writ shall be served upon the said Officer, or left at the Goal or Prison with any of the Under Officers, Under-Keepers, or Deputy of the said Officers or Keepers, that the said Officer or Officers, his or their Under Officers, Under-Keepers or Deputies, shall within three dayes after the Service thereof as aforesaid (unless the Commitment aforesaid were for Treason, or Felony, plainly and specially expressed in the Warrant of Commitment) upon payment or Tender of the Charges of bringing the said Prisoner to be Ascertained by the Judge or Court that Awarded the same, and Endorsed upon the said Writ, not exceeding Twelve-pence per Mile, and upon Security given by his own Bond to pay the Charges of carrying back the Prisoner, if he shall be Remanded by the Court or Judge, to which he shall be brought according to the true intent of this present Act, and that he will not make any Escape by the way, make Return of such Writ; and bring, or cause to be brought the Body of the Party so Committed or Restrained, unto, or before the Chief Justice, or any other of the Justices of the Superiour Court; And shall then likewise certifie the true Causes of his Detainer or Imprisonment, unless the Commitment of the said Party be in any place beyond the distance of Twenty Miles from the place or places where such Court or Person is or shall be Residing: and if beyond the distance of Twenty Miles, and not above One Hundred Miles, then within the space of Ten days, and if beyond the distance of One hundred Miles, then within the space of Twenty days, after such the delivery aforesaid, and not longer.

**And to the Intent** that no Sheriff, Goaler or other Officer, may pretend Ignorance of the Import of any such Writ.

**Be it Enacted by the Authority aforesaid.**

*Writs of Habeas Corpus and the Proceedings thereon in vacation time.*

That all such Writs shall be Signed by the person that Awards the same; & if any person or persons, shall be or stand Committed or Detained as aforesaid, for any Crime, unless for Felony or Treason, plainly expressed in the Warrant of Commitment, in the Vacation time, and out of Term; it shall and may be lawful to and for the person or persons so committed or detained (other than persons convict, or in Execution) by Legal Process or any one on his or their behalf, to appeal or complain to one or more of Their Majesties Justices of the Superiour Court, and the said Justice or Justices upon view of the Copy or Copies of the Warrant or Warrants of Commitment and detainer; or otherwise upon Oath made, that such Copy or Copies were denied to be given by such person or persons in whose custody the Prisoner or prisoners is or are detained, are hereby Authorized and Required upon request made in Writing by such person or persons, or any on his, her, or their behalf attested and subscribed by two Witnesses who were present at the Delivery of the same, to award and Grant an *Habeas Corpus* under the Seal of the said Court, to be Directed to the Officer or Officers

Officers, in whose Custody the Party so Committed or Detained shall be, Returnable immediately before the said Court, Justice, or Justices; and upon Service thereof as aforesaid, the Officer, or Officers, his or their Under Officer, or Under Officers, Under Keeper or Under Keepers, or Deputy, in whose Custody the Party is so Committed or Detained, shall within the times respectively before Limited, bring such Prisoner or Prisoners before the said Justice, before whom the said Writ is made Returnable; and in case of his Absence, before any other of them; with the Return of such Writ, & the true Causes of the Commitment & Detainer; & thereupon within two days after the Party shall be brought before the said Court, Justice or Justices, the said Court, or Justice, before whom the Prisoner shall be brought as aforesaid, shall Discharge the said Prisoner from his Imprisonment, taking his or their Recognizance, with one or more Surety, or Sureties in any Sum, according to their Discretions, having Regard to the Quality of the Prisoner, and nature of the Offence, for his or their Appearance in the said Superiour Court, the Term following, or at the next Assizes, Sessions or General Goal Delivery, within or for such County, or place where the Commitment was, or where the Offence was Committed, or in such other Court where the said Offence is properly Cognizable, as the Case shall Require; and then shall Certifie the said Writ, with the Return thereof, and the said Recognizance or Recognizances, into the said Court where such Appearance is to be made; unless it shall appear unto the said Court or Justice, that the Party so Committed, is Detained upon a Legal Process, Order or Warrant out of some Court that hath Jurisdiction of Criminal Matters, or by some Warrant, Signed and Sealed with the Hand and Seal of any of the said Justices, or some Justice or Justices of the Peace for such Matters or Offences, for the which by the Law the Prisoner is not Bailable.

**Provided always, and be it Enacted**, That if any person shall have wilfully neglected by the space of two whole Terms after his Imprisonment, to pray a *Habeas Corpus* for his Enlargement; such Person so wilfully neglecting, shall not have any *Habeas Corpus* to be Granted in vacation time, in pursuance of this Act.

*persons neglecting two Terms to pray a Habeas Corpus shall have none in vacation time, in pursuance of this Act.*

**And be it further Enacted by the authority aforesaid**, That if any Officer or Officers, his or their Under Officer or Under Officers, Under-Keeper or Under-Keepers, or Deputy, shall neglect or refuse to make the Returns aforesaid, or to bring the Body or Bodys of the Prisoner or Prisoners, according to the Command of the said Writ, within the Respective Times aforesaid, or upon Demand made by the Prisoner or Person in his behalf, shall Refuse to Deliver, or within the Space of Six Hours after Demand, shall not Deliver to the Person so Demanding, a True Copy of the Warrant or Warrants, of Commitment, and Detainer of such Prisoner; which he & they are hereby Required to Deliver accordingly, all & every the Head Goalers & Keepers of such Prisons, & such other Person in whose Custody the Prisoner shall be Detained, shall for the First Offence Forfeit to the Prisoner or Party grieved, the sum of Fifty Pounds; & for the Second Offence, the Sum of One Hundred Pounds; and shall and is hereby made incapable to

*officers how to be proceeded against for not obeying such Writts.*

hold

first Offence; And any after Recovery or Judgment at the Suit of a party grieved for any Offence after the First Judgment shall be a sufficient Conviction to bring the Officers or person within the said Penalty for the second Offence.

*Reasons set at large not to be Recommitted but by Order of Court*

**And for the prevention** of unjust vexation by reiterated Commitments for the same Offence, **Be it Enacted by the authority aforesaid**, That no person or persons, which shall be delivered or set at large upon any *Habeas Corpus*, shall at any time hereafter be again Imprisoned or Committed for the same Offence, by any person or persons whatsoever, other than by the Legal Order and Process of such Court wherein he or they shall be Bound by Recognizance to appear, or other Court having Jurisdiction of the Cause: And if any other person or persons shall knowingly contrary to this Act, Recommit or Imprison, or knowingly procure or cause to be Recommitted or Imprisoned for the same Offence, or pretended Offence, any person or persons delivered or set at large as aforesaid, or be knowingly aiding or assisting therein, then he or they shall Forfeit to the Prisoner or Party grieved, the Sum of Two Hundred Pounds, any colourable pretence, or variation in the Warrant or Warrants of Commitment notwithstanding, to be Recovered as aforesaid.

*Persons Committed for Treason or Felony shall be Indicted the next Term or let to Bayl.*

**Provided always, & be it further Enacted** That if any person or persons shall be Committed for High Treason or Felony, plainly and specially expressed in the Warrant of Commitment, upon his Prayer or Petition in open Court, the first week of the Term or first day of the Sessions of Oyer & Terminer, or General Goal Delivery, to be brought to his Tryal, shall not be Indicted some time to the next Term, Sessions of Oyer & Terminer, or General Goal Delivery after such Commitment, it shall and may be lawful to and for the Justices of the Superiour Court, & Justices of Oyer and Terminer or General Goal Delivery and they are hereby Required upon motion to them made in Open Court the last day of the Term, Sessions or Goal Delivery, either by the Prisoner, or any one in his behalf, to set at Liberty the Prisoner upon Bail, unless it appear to the Justices, upon Oath made, that the Witnesses for the King could not be produced the same Term, Sessions or General Goal Delivery: And if any person or persons Committed as aforesaid, upon his Prayer or Petition in Open Court the first week of the Term or first day of the Sessions of Oyer and Terminer, and General Goal Delivery, to be brought to his Tryal, shall not be Indicted and Tried the Second Term, Sessions of Oyer and Terminer, or General Goal Delivery after his Commitment, or upon his Tryal shall be Acquitted, he shall be Discharged from his Imprisonment. **Provided always** That nothing in this Act shall extend to Discharge out of Prison, any person Charged in Debt, or other Action, or with Process in any Civil Cause; but that after he shall be Discharged of his Imprisonment for such his Criminal Offence, he shall be kept in Custody according to the Law, for such other Suit. Provided

## Habeas Corpus Act

**Provided always, and be it Enacted by the Authority aforesaid.** That if any of their Majesties Subjects shall be committed to any Prison, or in Custody of any Officer or Officers whatsoever, for any Criminal, or supposed Criminal Matter, that the said Person shall not be Removed from the said Prison and Custody, into the Custody of any other Officer or Officers, unless it be by *Habeas Corpus*, or some other Legal Writ, or where the Prisoner is delivered to the Constable, or other Inferiour Officer, to carry such Prisoner to some Common Goal; or where any Person is Sent by Order of any Judge of Assize, or Justice of the Peace, to any Common Work-House, or House of Correction, or where the Prisoner is Removed from one Prison or Place to another within the same County, in order to his or her Tryal, or Discharge in due course of Law, or in case of sudden Fire or Infection, or other necessity: and if any person or persons shall after such Commitment aforesaid, Make out and Sign, or Countersign any Warrant or Warrants for such Removal aforesaid contrary to this Act; as well he that Makes or Signs, or Countersigns such Warrant or Warrants, as the Officer or Officers that Obey or Execute the same, shall suffer and Incur the Pains and Forfeitures in this Act before mentioned, both for the First and second Offence respectively, to be recovered in manner aforesaid by the Party grieved.

**Provided also, and be it further Enacted by the authority aforesaid.** That it shall and may be Lawful to and for any Prisoner and Prisoners as aforesaid, to Move and Obtain his or their *Habeas Corpus*. And if the said Justices for the time being, or any of them, in or out of Court, upon view of the Copy or Copies of the Warrant or Warrants of Commitment or Detainer, or upon Oath made that such Copy or Copies were denied as aforesaid, shall deny any Writ of *Habeas Corpus* by this Act Required to be granted, being moved for as aforesaid, they shall severally Forfeit to the Prisoner or Party grieved, the Sum of One Hundred Pounds, to be Recovered in manner aforesaid.

*Penalty, &c. for denying an Habeas Corpus.*

**Provided always, and be it Enacted,** That no Person or Persons shall be Sued, Impleaded, Molested or Troubled for any OFFENCE against this ACT, unless the Party Offending be Sued or Impleaded for the same, within two years at the most after such time wherein the Offence shall be Committed, in case the Party grieved shall not be then in Prison, and if he shall be in Prison, then within the space of two years after the Decease of the Person Imprisoned, or his or her Delivery out of Prison, which shall first happen.

*Prosecution for Offences within what time to be made*

**And to the Intent** no person may avoid his Tryal at the Assizes, or General Goal Delivery, by procuring his removal before the Assizes at such time as he cannot be brought back to receive his Tryal there.

**Be it Enacted.** That after the Assizes proclaimed for or within that County where the Prisoner is detained, no person shall be removed from the Common Goal, upon any *Habeas Corpus* granted in pursuance of this Act: but upon any such *Habeas Corpus* shall be brought before the Justices of Assize in open Court, who are thereupon to do what to Justice shall appertain.

Provided nevertheless, that after the Assizes are ended, any person or persons detained, may have his or her *Habeas Corpus* according to the direction and intention of this Act.

**And be it also Enacted by the Authority aforesaid,**

That if any Information, Suit, or Action shall be brought or exhibited against any person or persons for any Offence committed or to be committed against the form of this Law; It shall be lawful for such Defendants to plead the general Issue, *That they are not Guilty*, or that *they owe nothing*, and to give such special matter in Evidence to the Jury that shall try the same; which matter being pleaded, had been good and sufficient matter in Law to have discharged the said Defendant or Defendants against the said Information, Suit, or Action; and the said matter shall be then as available to him or them, to all Intents and purposes, as if he or they had sufficiently pleaded, set forth or alledged the said matter in Bar or Discharge of such Information, Suit, or Action.

## AN ACT,

### For the Reviving of An Act for continuing of the Local Laws. And one other Act, for sending of Souldiers to the Relief of the Neighbouring Provinces and Colonies.

WHereas at the Session of this Court in *June* last past: An Act was made, Entituled an Act For continuing the Local Laws to stand in Force, till *November* the Tenth One Thousand Six Hundred Ninety and Two, which Act is near Expired; And Forasmuch as Provision in many Cases is not yet made.

**Be it therefore Ordained by the Governour Council & Representatives in General Court Assembled. And by the Authority of the same.**

That the Said Act and every part of it, Be and hereby is revived and Continued in full Force to all intents, and Purposes from and after the Said Tenth Day of *November*, and shall so Continue until the General Assembly shall take further Order.

**And Whereas** at the aforesaid Session one Other Act was Made, Entituled, an Act for Transporting of part of the *Militia* of the Province or Obliging them to March to the Relief of the Neighbouring Provinces or Colonies, which Act is also near Expired. And Forasmuch as in this time of War there may happen Frequent Occasions for relief to be given unto the Neighbouring Provinces.

**It is therefore Further Enacted by the Authority aforesaid**

That the Said Act and every part of it be and hereby is revived and Continued in full Force to all intents and Purposes from and after the Expiration of the Six Months in Said Act Mentioned, and shall so continue unto the First Day of the Sessions of this Court, which shall be in *May* next, and no longer.

## FINIS

www.ingramcontent.com/pod-product-compliance
Lightning Source LLC
Chambersburg PA
CBHW032237080426
42735CB00008B/899